EVERYDAY SEAFOOD NATHAN OUTLAW

From the simplest fish to a seafood feast,
100 recipes for home cooking

Foreword by
Jamie Oliver

Photography by
David Loftus

quadrille

Foreword

It's a great honor to write the foreword for this beautiful book, especially as one of the best meals I've had this year was at Nathan's restaurant in Port Isaac. I've only known Nathan for the past few years, but boy, is he an infectious soul. He's a massive softie with a big heart, and one of the nicest guys in the restaurant industry. Our dads are both chefs, and that's probably what's given us the same level of pride for how we behave within the industry, as well as instilling in us an approach to recipe writing that ensures cooking is inclusive and accessible.

That is exactly what Nathan has achieved in this gorgeous book. His honest and uncomplicated approach speaks volumes in these pages. He's a tall boy with a big presence, but his food is beautifully delicate, thoughtfully presented, and at its core, embraces simple, clean, balanced flavors.

For me, this is a real genre buster of a book. Often people are nervous about cooking with seafood, but there's no need to be. On these pages you'll find incredible, modern, and exciting dishes, and totally do-able techniques that will serve you well for the rest of your life. Read through all the handy up-front info to get you in the right spirit, then pick your recipes and get cooking.

Mr. Outlaw certainly isn't messing about, and as well as everything looking and sounding phenomenal, he's definitely got all the bases covered. From some of the quickest most delicate raw dishes—which I think are my favorites—to twists on the classics, such as Crab Scotch quail eggs or Cod and ox cheek stew. Most are super economical if you're buying seasonally, then there's a few things that are a bit naughtier— Barbecued jerk lobster with coconut rice I'm looking at you! There's a whole lot to choose from.

Without doubt, Nathan is one of Britain's most devoted chefs, but because we like to pigeonhole people, we think that he's only about seafood, and although he probably would have married a mermaid should he have had access to one, the desserts in this book are totally delicious, too.

Finally, in crafting this book, Nathan has worked with the lovely David Loftus, one of the best food photographers on the planet, and another of my favorite people in the industry, so you can be sure that every photo will inspire you in an instant.

Nice one mate.
Jamie Oliver

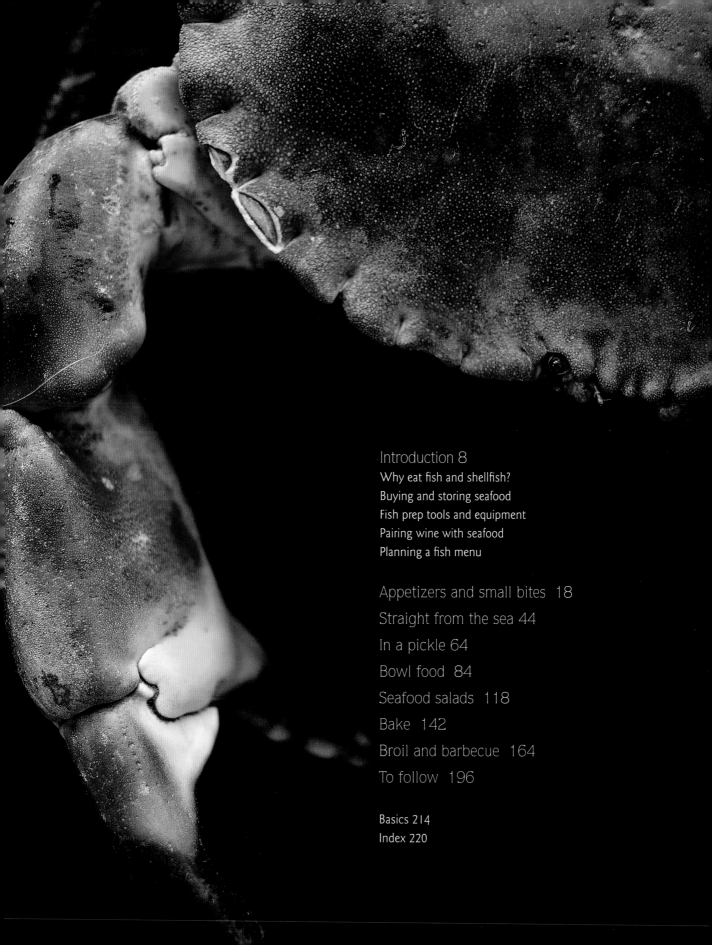

Introduction 8
Why eat fish and shellfish?
Buying and storing seafood
Fish prep tools and equipment
Pairing wine with seafood
Planning a fish menu

Appetizers and small bites 18

Straight from the sea 44

In a pickle 64

Bowl food 84

Seafood salads 118

Bake 142

Broil and barbecue 164

To follow 196

Basics 214
Index 220

Introduction

Seafood is the best convenience food ever! That's a bold statement, but it's true. Most seafood will cook within minutes—much faster than any ready prepared meal—and that, for me, is what makes it such a great choice for everyday meal occasions. I wanted to write this book to unlock the myth that seafood is a tricky thing to deal with: it's not. Follow my recipes and you will realize just how easy it is to cook.

Each recipe has been tested to make sure it can be cooked successfully at home—taking into account timing, availability of ingredients, and the equipment needed. I've done this personally, so I know the recipes work, and that you'll be able to follow them easily. The biggest single piece of advice I can give you is to read through the method before you start to cook, especially with the slightly more ambitious dishes.

The recipes are a collection of my take on classics from far and wide, with the simple approach to seafood that I'm known for. I've made sure the ingredients are accessible, and can be bought easily, because I don't want you to be put off by long lists of unfamiliar items.

However, the most significant point about the ingredients is that all the fish and shellfish used in these recipes is sustainable at the time of writing. The importance of sustainability is something I cannot stress enough. Please ask questions when you are buying. Any fish market or supplier worth your custom will have an acute awareness of sustainability and know where their seafood has come from. If they can't answer your questions, don't buy from them.

Once you become more confident, I hope you'll treat my recipes as a guide rather than stick to them. Feel free to play around with different fish and flavorings. It gives me such pride and pleasure when someone tells me they've tried a recipe from my book and then cooked it differently next time, adding this or that, and it tasted just as good... or better!

The recipes can be scaled up or down to suit your needs, so don't be put off if a recipe serves four, and there's just two of you. Just halve the quantities, or double or triple them for a crowd. It will be fine.

And finally, although this book will look lovely on your coffee table, I would much rather see it in the kitchen covered in splatters of food. I've written it to be used, so please go ahead... and enjoy!

Why eat fish and shellfish?

Apart from the fact that very fresh seafood tastes wonderful, there are many health benefits. Current guidelines suggest that we should eat at least two portions of fish a week. Not enough if you ask me! Fish is an excellent source of protein, vitamins, and minerals. Oily fish has the significant added bonus of being rich in omega-3 fatty acids, which help to keep our heart, joints, skin, and eyes healthy. And some of the smaller oily fish can be eaten whole, so they provide a particularly rich source of calcium and phosphorus.

For those who need to follow a low fat diet, the obvious choice is white fish, although not cooked in batter or bread crumbs. Shellfish is also low in fat, and a good source of zinc, iodine, copper, and selenium. Mussels, oysters, and crab provide a fair amount of omega-3 fatty acids too.

However, we need to set a few limits on the amount of oily fish we consume, as they sometimes contain low levels of pollutants, which can build up in the body. It is suggested that we should eat no more than four portions of oily fish per week. For anyone who is pregnant or breastfeeding, this reduces to two portions per week.

Porgy, bass, turbot and brown crabmeat may also contain low levels of pollutants, so it makes sense to eat these in moderation too. Swordfish is not featured in my book, but I should warn you that it can contain significant levels of mercury, and should be restricted to a maximum of two portions per week. Anyone who is pregnant or breastfeeding should avoid swordfish altogether.

You are now forewarned! But I doubt whether any of you are planning to eat fish at every meal, so these issues are unlikely to be a problem.

Buying and storing seafood

It goes without saying that you should buy the freshest fish available to you. It could be that you are lucky enough to have a "proper" fish market on your doorstep, or maybe even access to the fishermen themselves. If not, you will find that some of the better supermarkets now employ trained staff on their fish counters, so don't be reticent to buy from them. Remember to take an insulated bag with you to bring the fish home in; it will keep that much fresher.

Always take a look around the place you're buying from. Make sure it's clean and that the fish is displayed well. Also check out those behind the counter. They should be confident, and handle their fish and shellfish cleanly and carefully. And they must be able to answer any questions you have about the fish they are selling. If they can't, it's best to give the place a wide berth.

All fish and seafood should smell of the ozone, rather than "fishy." If it smells at all unpleasant, don't buy it! Make sure that whole fish look good. They should be intact, with no visible damage to any part. Eyes should be bright and clear, gills should be vivid red, and any scales that you expect to be there, should be in place. Flat fish should be firm and have some sea slime on the surface. Oily fish should have retained their natural color, and be vibrant, not dull.

In the case of shellfish, you will also need to check on their status. Molluscs need to be alive when you buy them. If clams, cockles, mussels, or oysters have open shells, tap them firmly, and if they don't close readily, don't buy, as this indicates that they are no longer alive.

One exception to the "live" rule is scallops, which often come to the market ready prepared and cut from the shell. However, they should still smell ozony and sweet. Also, make sure they are firm and haven't been left to soak. If any of these criteria aren't met, leave them in the store!

When buying lobsters and crabs, again, they should be alive. Check there are no bubbles coming from their mouths, as this is a sign that they are stressed, and it will affect the quality of their meat. Lobsters should have long antennae; short ones suggest the lobster has been stored for a long while and has either begun to eat itself or been eaten by others.

Finally, the cephalopods—squid and octopus—really need to be eaten within a couple of days of being caught. Their eyes should be bright and the creatures should be intact, with no signs of changing color to pink, as this suggests they have seen better days.

If you've found a bargain or someone has brought you lots of freshly caught fish, don't turn it away—most fish freezes well.

Ideally, seafood should be eaten within 24 hours of buying. Store it wrapped in a damp cloth in the coldest area of the fridge. Don't let it sit in water though, as this will impair the flavor. The fridge needs to be between 32°F and 35°F [0°C and 2°C]. If you can, cover the wrapped fish with a layer of fresh ice—don't let it touch the fish directly as this will cause "freezer burn." Stored carefully on the bone, most fish will be fine for several days.

If you know that you won't be eating the fish within a few days, take it off the bone, make sure it's completely dry, then wrap it tightly in plastic wrap and put it in the freezer as soon as you can. It will keep quite happily for up to 2 months. In the case of lobster and crab, cook before freezing, cool, and wrap securely before putting into the freezer. Always allow fish and seafood to defrost slowly in the fridge before cooking.

Fish prep tools and equipment

Buying equipment for cooking can be daunting—there's so much out there to choose from. I've put together a list of the items I use day in, day out, and have been using for the last twenty years. Remember though, this is my personal choice, and you may already have, or prefer to buy, something different. That's fine, but please make sure you buy good quality products. Trust me, if you skimp, you'll only be buying again soon, which is not only frustrating, it can end up costing you more...

Knives

I strongly recommend investing in a selection of good knives for your kitchen. The following are the ones I use all the time:

Filleting knife There are many types of filleting knife on the market, with various uses. I use a thin, semi-flexible bladed one. You can get some that are very flexible, but they are not easy to sharpen. If you buy a good quality filleting knife, it should last a lifetime.

Cook's knife I tend to use two cook's knives. One has a 10 in [25 cm] long blade. The other is heavier with a 12 in [30 cm] blade—it needs to be, because I use it for bashing lobsters and crabs and steaking fish. It's much safer to use a heavy knife for jobs like this so that it doesn't bounce off and injure you. I use the lighter 10 in [25 cm] knife for slicing and chopping, and I keep the blade razor sharp.

Paring knife A good paring knife is a must. Don't be tempted to buy one that's too big, or you'll find it clumsy to handle when you are peeling garlic or an onion, for example. Keep it nice and sharp at all times. Apart from preparing veg and fruit, I also use a small paring knife for scaling fish, but do be careful if you try this—it's much safer to use a proper fish scaler.

Serrated knife A strong serrated knife is most useful for cutting off fish heads. When I'm dealing with bigger fish, I always cut the head off first, as I find it gives you more control when filleting.

Oyster knife It took me years to find an oyster knife that I like to use. The one I own and love has a wooden handle, and a firm but short blade. I always keep it sharpened, so it slices through the muscle cleanly, giving a very presentable oyster.

Firm bladed boning knife This is a personal preference and technically not a correct use of this knife, but I find a boning knife is the best one to use for opening scallops. If you're planning to open lots of scallops, I'd suggest investing in one.

Sharpener

I've always been terrible at keeping my knives sharp. It's not the most interesting of jobs to do in the kitchen. However, I had a revelation when I discovered a sharpener with a guided sharpening wheel on it. I'm not really one for gadgets, but since I've been using this, my knives are always sharp and ready to rock. A great investment!

Rubber mallet

I always use a rubber mallet when I want to steak fish into portions.

Hitting the heavy 12 in [30 cm] cook's knife with the mallet leaves you with a very clean and precise cut.

Microplane grater

This is probably one of the most frequently used pieces of kit in my kitchen. These graters are worth every penny, and if looked after properly should last you for ages. We use them for zesting citrus fruit and grating cheese, garlic, chocolate, etc. Trust me, once you begin using one, it will become an integral part of your life in the kitchen. One word of warning though: they are very sharp, so mind your fingers!

Mandoline

A Japanese mandoline is a good friend to have in your kitchen. I use one a lot for finely slicing vegetables, such as fennel, for salads and pickles. Again, be very careful. Fingers and mandolines don't mix!

Long-handled dessert spoon

This has a few, important functions. Firstly, it's ideal for scooping a scallop out of its shell because the bowl is made of thin, rounded metal, almost the same shape as the rounded side of a scallop shell. Secondly, I use it when picking crabs. Using both handle and bowl ends, these spoons can get into every crevice of a crab shell, enabling me to prise out every last piece of that fantastic crabmeat. Also, they tend not to break the cartilage too much, and you don't want that in your crabmeat. Of course, these spoons are also useful for tasting as you cook, and for serving up when you are aiming to get the presentation precise.

Pin-boning tweezers

These are an absolutely essential item for your fish prepping kit. Make sure you buy a pair that have no flex to them. The flexible ones seem to struggle to grab smaller bones.

Cutting boards

It is worth investing in a good quality blue plastic cutting board if you plan to do lots of fish prep. When you have finished using it, always wash the board with cold water rather than hot, as hot water will cook the remaining debris and make the board smell.

Always dry the board thoroughly before putting it away too, as again it will smell if you don't.

For other food prep, I love using my large wooden cutting boards, but I really wouldn't recommend wood for preparing fish, as it is very difficult to clean the fish debris from. Never, ever be tempted to put your wooden cutting board into the dishwasher as it does very strange things to them!

Small stainless steel bowls

These are not expensive to buy, but they are so useful to have on hand for all sorts of purposes, from holding pre-prepped ingredients, to mixing small quantities of dressing, and storing food in the fridge. Get several—you'll be reaching for them all the time!

Strainers

I would recommend having a choice of strainers in your kitchen. It just makes it easier to achieve the desired result. A fine strainer is best for sauces and stocks. A slightly coarser strainer is great for purées and bread crumbs. A large conical strainer is useful for straining fish stocks.

Heat resistant spatula

A good quality, flexible, heatproof rubber spatula is a great kitchen tool. Ideal for mixing, it gets right into the edges of the pan or bowl you're using, and enables you to scrape out every last bit when you have finished.

Electronic digital scales

Having electronic digital scales on hand in your kitchen makes life that much easier. Try to get scales that have a decent sized platform and weigh in American and metric for both dry goods and liquids. Take care of them though. They are quite delicate and feature at the top of our "Chef, the equipment is broken" list!

Electric blender/processor

Once again, it pays long term to buy robust, good quality small electrical appliances. If you want soups and purées that are really fine, a powerful electric blender or food processor is a must. Always be careful when putting hot liquid into a blender though, as the machine has a tendency to throw the liquid up at you as hot air builds up.

Electric mixer

I don't often use my mixer when I'm preparing fish, but it's really handy for desserts. If you are thinking of buying one, I would recommend a KitchenAid. Yes, they are expensive, but they are robust, and look pretty snazzy too.

Pans

There are loads of pans on the market, but if you want a really good long-term investment, choose the ones with heavy bottoms and tight-fitting lids. If they're ovenproof, even better. A thicker bottomed pan helps cook food more evenly and gives you lots of residual heat when you take it off the heat source. They are also good to braise in, hence the need for a tight-fitting lid.

For pan-frying fish, a good quality nonstick pan is essential as far as I'm concerned. You need to look after it though. Don't leave it on the heat as you might a cast iron pan. If you do, after a while the coating will burn off... you really don't want bits of nonstick coating in your food.

Oven and grill pans

Whether you are broiling, grilling, or baking, you need to invest in some good quality pans. If they are too thin, they'll buckle under the heat, and the food won't cook evenly. Buy a range of sizes—from pans big enough to hold a couple of fish fillets, up to one big enough to take a whole fish. If you buy cast iron, make sure that you dry them well after washing, or they will go rusty. A little tip: I always wash and dry my pans, then finish them in a warm oven to make sure they are thoroughly dry.

Steamer

Steaming fish shows off the freshness of the fish, and the purity of its flavor. It's one of my favorite ways to cook fish. A steamer is a great piece of kit, and worth every penny. If you're very fortunate, you may have an integrated steamer in your oven. Otherwise, you can buy one to use on the stove. You might choose to get one of the tall electric steamers, but I prefer to use a simple metal steamer.

Pairing wine with seafood

Damon Little, Sommelier, Restaurant Nathan Outlaw

There's nothing better than discovering a sensational new wine—one that ticks all the boxes, and every sip is absolute bliss. If it's then paired successfully to a recipe, the pleasure is heightened even further.

If you are feeling a little adventurous and fancy trying something new, consider buying wine from an independent wine merchant. Often the people who work there will have tasted most of the wines on offer, and will be able to give you sound advice and make suitable suggestions.

Higher price does not necessarily indicate better quality wine, as you may be buying a very expensive wine that is not ready to drink, and could therefore be rather unpleasant. Having said that, please be aware that if you purchase a wine for say, $7.50, you have to factor in federal excise tax. After you deduct the cost of the bottle, transport, the retailer's mark-up, and the producer's mark-up, eventually the liquid in the bottle is worth only a few pennies. And you probably have to add state and possibly city sales tax to the cost of the bottle... Are you really going to enjoy that?

If you are not sure where to begin when it comes to choosing wine to drink with seafood, my advice would be to start by having your favorite wine with your favorite recipe. You'll get to know which combinations are pleasurable, and which are not so good. Most of us would taste the wine before eating, so sip the wine again after a mouthful of food, and see how the food affects the wine and vice versa.

There are many, if not hundreds, of wines that work well with seafood beyond the familiar classic partners, such as Muscadet or Champagne with freshly shucked oysters. The most successful pairings occur when the structure of the wine works in harmony with the structure of the recipe. The structure of wine can be broken down into body and flavor intensity, acidity, and sweetness.

Body and flavor intensity

A bold dish requires a bold wine. The most practical way to determine the body of a wine, is to compare the mouth-feel to that of water, milk or cream, which would translate to light, medium, and full-bodied. Match the textures of your recipe with the body of your wine. If the dish is bold, then the flavors of wine should be bold.

Acidity

You can determine the level of acidity in wine by assessing the effect on salivation. The next time you taste white wine, tilt your head forward and down with your lips closed, to ascertain how much saliva builds up in your mouth. Acidity in wine is detected towards the back and at the sides of your tongue. Acidity in wine pairs well with fatty or oily foods, as it has a palate-cleansing "cutting through" effect, which counteracts the richness of the food. Note that acidity in food reduces the effect of acidity in wine.

Sweetness

This an incredibly objective aspect of wine. You may have a dry aromatic wine offering flavors of ripe peaches and apricots, which in our minds resembles sweetness, yet it is still a dry wine based on actual residual sugar. The sweetness level in wine is detected at the very tip of your tongue.

Sweet food reduces the sweetness in wine, so the sweetness in wine should either be equal to, or preferably a little higher than that of the dish. Sweetness in wine is also a fantastic complement to salty food, so a sweet wine works with blue cheese. Try Sauternes with Roquefort or foie gras.

Other characteristics

Be aware that the bitterness in food increases the bitterness in wine.

Also, heat generated from chiles can increase the perception of bitterness, astringency, and acidity—and you will also feel the heat from the alcohol causing a slight burn.

Red wine with fish?

We have had many successful red wine pairings with seafood. There are numerous low tannin, light-bodied reds available. The reason those reds have a lighter body and lighter tannic structure, is because the actual skin of the grape is much thinner than others. For example, Gamay and Pinot Noir will be lighter than Cabernet Sauvignon and Merlot. One of the most sensational combinations is salmon and beets with an earthy, spicy Pinot Noir that has good acidity.

Wine and seafood varieties

When choosing wine, you need to consider the different characteristics of fish and shellfish varieties.

Flat white fish: Dover sole, lemon sole, flounder, dab, halibut, turbot, brill, skate
These range in density, but generally have a light flavor. Minerality is key when choosing your matching wine. For the lighter style of flat fish like sole or flounder, pair floral wines that offer orchard fruit (apple/pear). Of course, hints of citrus are an advantage too.

Round white fish: porgy, cod, pollack, haddock, hake, John Dory, lingcod, monkfish, whiting
These have slightly more flavor than flat white fish, but pair well with similar wines. Wines with hints of citrus and orchard fruit work best.

White fish with slightly oily flesh: mullet, bass
Wines produced on marl (marine fossil soil), such as Jura wines, complement the subtle earthiness of these fish, but acidity is of the essence here to cut through the oiliness of the fish.

Oily fish: mackerel, sardine, herring, salmon, steelhead trout
These stronger flavored fish call for aromatic wines with higher acidity to cut through their oiliness. Alsace wines are good options, especially Riesling. Avoid red wine with tannins, as it may cause a metallic reaction.

Cephalopods: squid, octopus
These have a delicate flavor and a soft texture. The light, white pepperiness of Grüner Veltliner backed up by the hints of soft stone fruit work particularly well with cephalopods.

Molluscs: clams, razor clams, cockles, mussels, oysters
As these are high in minerals, avoid serving red wines with tannins, as it may cause a metallic reaction. The ultimate pairings include Champagne, Chablis, and Muscadet, all of which are crisp, zingy, and mineral.

Shellfish: scallops, crab, lobster
These are usually cooked with butter, or have a buttery sauce or dressing, so fuller bodied, buttery wines are an excellent choice. Try a white Burgundy from the Côte de Beaune. Very fresh shellfish has an underlying sweetness, which could be complemented by an off-dry style of wine, or a crisp, aromatic Albariño from Galicia, Spain; Gisborne from Eastland, New Zealand; or Montevideo from Uruguay.

There may be several different fish and shellfish within a dish, plus vegetables, fruit, etc. to consider when you are choosing a wine. As a guideline, try and match the flavor of your wine to the strongest flavor of the dish, but consider how it will pair with the mildest flavor too.

Planning a fish menu

Sometimes it's hard to know what to cook and even more so when you have constraints on your time, or a party to cater for. Getting everything to balance in terms of flavors, textures, and effort involved takes some practice, so I've decided to give you a few pointers by suggesting five menus for different occasions using the recipes from the book. Scale the quantities up or down, according to the number you are serving, and add your own choice of veg, salad, and bread where necessary.

A quick dinner for two

You can rustle this up in less than an hour—perfect for a midweek after-work supper.

Smoked Mackerel & Pickled Vegetable Salad (page 141)
Haddock Baked in a Bag with Béarnaise Butter (page 152)
Pear Crumble with Earl Grey Chocolate Sauce (page 200)

A leisurely lunch for four

An ideal meal to serve when lunch can extend through the afternoon, or supper can go on through the evening, taking time between courses to chat and raise a glass.

Raw Salmon with Vodka, Orange, & Horseradish (page 48)
Soused Sea Robin, Red Pepper Ketchup, Arugula & Olive Salad (page 79)
Lemon Sole, Green Sauce Butter (page 177)
Rhubarb Sponge, Almond Cream, & Lemon Crème Fraîche (page 198)

A dinner to impress for six or more

For a special occasion, it's always good to come up with a menu that leaves you little to do at the last minute. This one works a treat.

Crab Scotch Quail Eggs with Watercress Mayonnaise (page 22)
Gin-cured Sea (Steelhead) Trout with Apple & Fennel (page 56)
Dressed Lobster with Herb Mayonnaise (page 128)
Cod & Ox Cheek Stew (page 114)
Warm Chocolate Tart "Black Pig" (page 203)

Outdoor summer meal for six or more

As far as I'm concerned, there's only one way to cook on a hot day – outside on the barbecue. Add a couple of salads, a dessert and a few drinks, relax and enjoy!

Shrimp, Chile, & Potato Salad (page 126)
Monkfish, Cauliflower Pickle, Ginger & Coriander Yogurt (page 188)
Mackerel with Barbecue Sauce (page 190)
Sea Robin with Fennel, Gherkin, & Olive Salad (page 194)
Elderflower Cream with Strawberry Sorbet (page 205)

A family buffet for eight to ten

For a buffet you need dishes that will happily sit on the table for a while, so it's easier if most of them are served at room temperature. I like to include a couple that can be warmed up easily too.

Shrimp Cocktail Quiche (page 26)
Hot-smoked Salmon Pâté, Whiskey Jelly (page 32)
Jacob's Favorite Cod Roe Dip (page 34)
Doom Bar Marinated Seafood (page 69)
Crab & Tomato Salad with Horseradish Dressing (page 124)
Sardine, Pepper, & Shallot Flatbreads (page 156)
Treacle & Raspberry Tart (page 210)

APPETIZERS & SMALL BITES

For this beautiful appetizer, make sure your crabmeat is in tip-top condition, as the dish really shows off its quality. Trust me, you will get a few wows when your guests, family, and friends try it. I like to serve it with a pile of lightly toasted sourdough.

Crab pâté with pink grapefruit

Serves 4 as an appetizer

10½ oz [300 g] white crabmeat (from a 1.5 kg [3¼ lb] freshly cooked crab)
Sea salt and freshly ground black pepper

For the pâté

7 oz [200 g] brown crabmeat, strained
1½ sheets of bronze gelatin
2 Tbsp brandy
A pinch of cayenne pepper
A pinch of ground cumin
⅞ cup [200 ml] heavy cream
2 Tbsp lime juice

For the pink grapefruit jelly

2½ sheets of bronze gelatin
1¼ cups [300 ml] freshly squeezed pink grapefruit juice (from about 2 grapefruit)
¼ cup [50 g] superfine sugar
A pinch of sea salt

To garnish

1 pink grapefruit, sectioned
Peppergrass cress
A drizzle of olive oil

To serve

Sourdough bread

Pick through your crabmeat, checking for any shell or cartilage to discard. Put the white crabmeat into a bowl, and season with salt and pepper to taste. Put 4 Tbsp into a small bowl for the garnish and refrigerate. Divide the rest equally between 4 small bowls or ramekins.

To make the pâté, soak the gelatin in a shallow dish of ice water for about 5 minutes to soften. Heat the brown crabmeat, brandy, and spices in a small pan over low heat. Simmer gently for a minute, then add the cream and heat through.

Remove the gelatin from the dish, and squeeze out the excess water, then add it to the brown crab, off the heat, stirring to melt. Transfer to a blender, and blend for 1 minute, adding the lime juice and a pinch of salt. Pass the mixture through a strainer into a pitcher, and pour it equally over the white crabmeat in the bowls. Place in the fridge to set.

While the crab pâté is setting, make the grapefruit jelly. Soak the gelatin in ice water, as above, to soften. Put the grapefruit juice, sugar, and a pinch of salt into a pan and bring to a boil. Remove the gelatin from the dish, and squeeze out the excess water, then add to the juice mixture, off the heat, stirring until fully melted. Leave to cool, but don't let it set.

When the pâté is set, pour the cooled, liquid jelly evenly over the surface, and return to the fridge to set.

Take the pâté out of the fridge around 20 minutes before serving to bring it to room temperature. Cut away the peel and pith from the grapefruit, and cut out the sections from between the membranes; cut these into smaller pieces.

To serve, spoon the reserved white crabmeat on top of the pâté. Add the grapefruit pieces, scatter over some cress, and drizzle with olive oil. Toast the sourdough and serve with the pâté.

Okay, so these little nibbles are not real Scotch eggs, but they are just as tasty in my opinion, and they work so well with the peppery watercress mayonnaise. If the idea of crab doesn't float your boat, we do a fabulous smoked fish version too—just replace the crab with smoked haddock and proceed in the same way.

Crab Scotch quail eggs with watercress mayonnaise

Makes 12; Serves 4
as an appetizer

For the crab mix
7 oz [200 g] fresh raw cod
  fillet, diced
½ cup [75 g] brown crabmeat,
  strained
Heaping 1¼ cups [200 g]
  white crabmeat, picked
Finely grated zest of 1 lemon
2 Tbsp chopped chives
Sea salt and freshly ground
  black pepper

For the eggs
14 quail eggs (includes
  2 extras in case of breakage)
¾ cup [100 g] all-purpose
  flour, for coating
2 medium (hen) eggs, beaten
3 slices [100 g] day-old bread,
  crumbed in a blender
Sunflower oil for deep-frying

For the watercress
  mayonnaise
2 egg yolks
¾ tsp English mustard
¼ cup [20 g] grated aged
  sharp Cheddar cheese
1½ Tbsp white wine vinegar
3 Tbsp watercress, chopped
1¼ cups [300 ml] sunflower
  oil

To serve
1 lemon, cut into wedges

Put the cod fillet into a food processor with a good pinch of salt and blend for 30 seconds. Add the brown crabmeat, and blend for an additional 30 seconds. Scrape into a bowl, and add the white crabmeat, lemon zest, chives, and seasoning. Mix together well, cover, and place in the fridge.

Place the quail eggs in a pan, cover with cold water, and bring to a boil over high heat. Meanwhile, get ready a bowl of ice water. As soon as the water begins to boil, take the eggs out of the pan, and plunge them into the ice water. Let cool, then peel the eggs.

Set up three bowls: one with flour, one with beaten eggs and one with bread crumbs. Using clean hands, carefully mold the crab mixture around each quail egg and pass through the flour, then the egg and finally the bread crumbs to coat. Put the coated eggs aside, or in the fridge if you are cooking them later.

To make the mayonnaise, put the egg yolks into a blender or small food processor with the mustard, grated cheese, wine vinegar, and watercress. Process for 1 minute, and then, with the motor still running, slowly pour in the oil. Once it is fully emulsified, stop the machine and season the mayonnaise with salt to taste. Transfer to a bowl, cover, and refrigerate.

When ready to serve, heat the oil in a deep-fat fryer or other suitable deep, heavy pan to 325°F [160°C]. Deep-fry the Scotch eggs in the hot oil, in batches as necessary, for about 3 minutes until golden. Drain on paper towels, and season with a little salt.

Spoon the watercress mayonnaise into a bowl. Place the Scotch eggs on a warm platter with the bowl of mayonnaise and lemon wedges.

Oysters and bacon are a great flavor combination. Their salty and rich flavors need something to cut them, and that's where the zingy dipping sauce comes in—it has a little kick from the chile too. A cucumber and fennel salad brings the whole dish together with its lovely fresh textures.

Pancetta-wrapped oyster fritters with cucumber and mint dipping sauce

Serves 4 as an appetizer

12 live Pacific oysters
3½ Tbsp olive oil
1 white onion, peeled and minced
½ fennel bulb, tough outer layer removed, minced
Scant 1¾ cups [100 g] fresh bread crumbs
2 Tbsp chopped mint
2 Tbsp chopped curly parsley
Finely grated zest and juice of 1 lime
12 thin slices of pancetta
Sea salt and freshly ground black pepper

For the dipping sauce

1 cucumber
1 shallot, peeled and minced
½ fennel bulb, tough outer layer removed, minced
A small bunch of mint, leaves picked and finely sliced
1 large green chile, seeded and minced
3 Tbsp fish sauce
3 Tbsp cider vinegar
3 Tbsp water

For the salad

1 cucumber
1 fennel bulb, tough outer layer removed
1 tsp toasted nigella seeds
Juice of 1 lime
A generous drizzle of extra virgin olive oil

Open the oysters and strain their juice through a muslin-lined strainer into a bowl. Chop the oysters, and then add them to the juices.

Heat a skillet over medium heat and add the olive oil. When it is hot, add the onion and fennel, and cook for about 5 minutes until softened. Transfer to a bowl, and allow to cool slightly.

Add the oysters and juice, bread crumbs, herbs, lime zest, and juice to the softened veg and mix well. Season with pepper (you won't need salt because the oysters have enough).

Divide the mixture into 12 even-sized balls and roll them into football shapes. Lay the pancetta slices on a board, and place an oyster ball on each one, then wrap in the pancetta.

Preheat your broiler to its highest setting. Oil the broiler pan, place the fritters on it, and set aside.

For the dipping sauce, halve, peel, and seed the cucumber, then cut into ¼-inch [5 mm] dice. Place in a bowl with all the other ingredients, and toss to mix. Divide between 4 small dishes and set aside.

For the salad, halve, peel, seed, and finely slice the cucumber. Finely slice the fennel, using a mandoline if you have one. Toss the cucumber, fennel, and nigella seeds together, season with a little salt, and dress with the lime juice and olive oil.

To cook the fritters, place them under the broiler and cook for 3 minutes on one side, then carefully turn them, and cook for another 3 minutes.

Divide the salad between 4 appetizer plates, and place a dish of dipping sauce on each one. Once the fritters are cooked, divide them between the plates and serve.

I love a good shrimp cocktail, who doesn't? This picnic quiche is a little nod to the 70s classic. It has the same flavors, but no limp lettuce or tasteless tomato. You can make a big one if you wish, or little canapé-sized ones as I sometimes do; just adjust the cooking time accordingly. Shrimp cocktail will never be the same again!

Shrimp cocktail quiche

Serves 6 as an appetizer

For the pastry

1⅞ cups [250 g] all-purpose flour
⅔ cup [150 g] unsalted butter, diced
1 tsp fine sea salt
2 tsp minced rosemary
1 large egg, beaten
3 Tbsp milk
Egg wash (1 egg yolk beaten with 2 Tbsp milk)

For the filling

15 raw tiger shrimp, peeled, deveined, and halved
3 large eggs
1¼ cups [300 ml] heavy cream
3½ Tbsp good quality tomato ketchup, ideally homemade (see page 219)
½ tsp Tabasco sauce
5 scallions, trimmed and sliced
10 cherry tomatoes, halved
¾ cup [50 g] Parmesan, freshly grated
Sea salt and freshly ground black pepper

To make the pastry, put the flour, butter, salt, and rosemary into a food processor, and process until the mixture resembles fine bread crumbs. Add the egg and milk, and pulse briefly until the dough comes together. Shape the pastry into a disc, wrap in plastic wrap, and rest in the fridge for at least 1 hour. Preheat your oven to 375°F [190°C].

Roll out the pastry on a lightly floured surface to ⅛ in [3 mm] thick, and use to line a loose-based rectangular tart or quiche pan, about 10-by-4-1½-in [25-by-10-by-3-cm], or a 7 in [18 cm] round pan, 1½ in [3 cm] deep.

Line the pastry case with a sheet of parchment paper, and add a layer of ceramic baking beans. Rest in the fridge for 15 minutes.

Bake the pastry case for 15 minutes, then lift out the paper and beans, and brush the pastry with egg wash. Return to the oven for 3 minutes, then remove, and set aside. Turn the oven down to 325°F [160°C].

For the filling, lightly beat the eggs, cream, tomato ketchup, and Tabasco together, and season with salt and pepper. Scatter the scallions and cherry tomatoes in the pastry case, followed by the shrimp, distributing them evenly. Pour on the egg and cream mixture, then sprinkle with the grated Parmesan. Bake for 25 to 30 minutes, until the custard is set and the pastry is golden.

Leave the quiche in the pan on a wire rack to cool a little before slicing. Either eat warm, or leave it to cool completely and take on a picnic.

I serve these crisp-fried fish bites on toothpicks on a platter with a dish of chili jam. They are great as a pre-dinner bite, or handed around at a party. Mullet is ideal for this sort of cooking, because it has a decent oily content that stops it drying out. Mackerel, sardines, and salmon are good alternatives. You'll probably have more chili jam than you need, but it will keep for a few weeks in the fridge in a sealed container, and is delicious with cheese and cold meats.

Crispy fried mullet, chili jam

Serves 4 as an appetizer, or up to 8 as a bite

14 oz [400 g] mullet fillet, skinned and pin-boned
2 Tbsp chopped cilantro
Finely grated zest of 1 lime
½ tsp ground cumin
½ tsp cayenne pepper
¾ cup [100 g] gluten-free self-rising flour
½ cup [120 ml] Cornish Pilsner or similiar beer
Sunflower oil for deep-frying
Sea salt and freshly ground black pepper

For the chili jam

1 red onion, peeled and minced
4 red peppers, cored, seeded and finely sliced
6 red chiles, seeded and finely sliced
3 garlic cloves, peeled and chopped
14 oz [400 g] canned plum tomatoes
1½ cups [300 g] soft brown sugar
⅔ cup [150 ml] red wine vinegar
2 lemongrass stalks, tough outer layers removed, minced

To serve

1 lime, cut into wedges

To make the chili jam, put all of the ingredients into a heavy-bottomed pan (I use a cast iron one) and add a pinch of salt. Bring to a boil, stirring to dissolve the sugar, then reduce the heat, and simmer gently, stirring occasionally, for about 45 minutes until the jam is well reduced. Once it starts to stick on the bottom of the pan, stir constantly over the heat until it looks like bubbling lava. Transfer to a bowl, and leave to cool. (Once cooled, the jam can be kept in the fridge in a sealed container.)

Cut the mullet into roughly 1½ in [4 cm] chunks. Mix the chopped cilantro, lime zest, cumin, cayenne, and a good pinch of salt together in a bowl. Add the mullet pieces and toss to mix. Leave to marinate for 30 minutes.

To make the batter, mix the flour and beer together until smooth. Heat the oil in a deep-fat fryer or other suitable deep, heavy-bottomed pan to 350°F [180°C]. Season the fish with salt and pepper.

You will need to cook the fish in 2 or 3 batches. One at a time, dip each chunk into the batter to coat, then carefully lower into the hot oil. Deep-fry for 3 to 4 minutes, until cooked and crispy. Gently lift the fish out and drain on paper towels. Keep warm while you cook the rest.

Sprinkle the fish chunks with a little salt and spear onto toothpicks. Serve immediately, on a platter, or individual plates with a bowl of chili jam and lime wedges on the side.

My version of the French brandade, using Cornish smoked haddock and saffron, may upset purists, but who cares—it tastes really good! It's versatile, too. You can dress it up in individual bowls to serve as a posh appetizer with toasted sourdough, or you can just whack it in the middle of the table with a pile of raw vegetables and everyone can dip away.

A Cornish style of smoked brandade

Serves 8 as an appetizer

18 oz [500 g] finest smoked haddock or smoked pollack, skinned and pin-boned

2 large baking potatoes, peeled

A pinch of saffron strands

1¼ cups [300 ml] whole milk

2 garlic cloves, peeled and minced

2 bay leaves

⅞ cup [200 ml] cold-pressed canola oil, plus a drizzle to finish

2 Tbsp flat-leaf parsley leaves, finely sliced

Juice of 1 lemon, or to taste

Sea salt and freshly ground black pepper

To serve

Sourdough bread, thickly sliced

Cut the potatoes into large even-sized chunks and place in a saucepan. Cover with water, and add salt and the saffron. Bring to a simmer, and cook for about 15 minutes until soft.

Meanwhile, pour the milk into another pan and add the garlic and bay leaves. Bring to a simmer over medium heat, then add the fish. Take the pan off the heat, and leave the fish to cook in the residual heat of the milk for 6 minutes. Remove the fish and flake into a food processor; reserve the milk.

Transfer the potatoes to a colander and leave them to drain and dry off for a few minutes. Meanwhile, gently warm the canola oil in a pan.

Purée the fish in the processor, then, with the motor running, slowly pour in the warm oil and the reserved milk through the funnel. Once it is all incorporated, add most of the parsley, saving a little for the garnish.

Add the potatoes to the mixture and blitz for 30 seconds. Finally, add most of the lemon juice, and a good sprinkling of pepper.

Scrape the brandade into a bowl and give it a good stir. Taste and adjust the seasoning, adding more lemon juice if required.

Just before serving, toast the sourdough slices. Serve the brandade topped with a drizzle of canola oil and the remaining parsley, with the toasted sourdough on the side.

Salmon and whiskey is a pairing I've been serving in various ways since I opened my first restaurant, Black Pig, in 2003. Good quality hot-smoked salmon is available from good delis, supermarkets, and online—it's well worth buying superior smoked fish, because the texture and flavor will be better. If whiskey isn't your thing, you could use the same recipe to create a beet jelly, swapping the whiskey for beet juice.

Hot-smoked salmon pâté, whiskey jelly

Serves 6 as an appetizer

For the pâté

14 oz [400 g] hot-smoked salmon, skinned
Finely grated zest and juice of 1 lime
3½ oz [100 g] full-fat cream cheese
⅔ cup [150 g] full-fat Greek yogurt
1 Tbsp creamed horseradish
Sea salt and freshly ground black pepper

For the whiskey jelly

2 sheets of bronze gelatin
⅞ cup [200 ml] Laphroaig single malt or similiar Scotch whiskey
3¼ Tbsp [40 g] superfine sugar

To serve

12 slices of rye bread
Grated zest of 1 lime

To make the pâté, put the hot-smoked salmon into a food processor with the lime juice and blitz for 20 seconds. Scrape down the sides of the bowl, and add the cream cheese, yogurt, horseradish, lime zest, and some salt and pepper. Blitz for 1 minute: you want the pâté to be almost smooth, with a little texture from the salmon. Divide between 6 ramekins or other small dishes, cover and refrigerate.

To make the jelly, soak the gelatin in a shallow dish of ice water for about 5 minutes to soften. Put the whiskey and sugar into a pan, and heat gently until the sugar has dissolved, and the liquor is almost at a simmer.

Remove the gelatin leaves from the dish, and squeeze out the excess water. Add to the whiskey, off the heat, and stir until melted. Leave to cool completely, but don't let it set.

Pour the cooled, liquid jelly evenly on top of the pâté and return to the fridge to set.

Take the pâté out of the fridge around 20 minutes before serving, so that it comes to room temperature.

When ready to eat, toast the rye bread. Sprinkle the lime zest over the pâté, and serve immediately, with the toast.

My son Jacob adores this dip. It was originally created as a bar snack to serve with drinks at Outlaw's Fish Kitchen in Port Isaac, Cornwall. and has been on the menu ever since. Easy to make, it's a great dish for a party and keeps well in the fridge for 3 to 4 days. I serve it topped generously with smoked paprika and garlicky olive oil, with a pile of warm flatbreads to tear and scoop up the dip. You should be able to get good smoked cod roe from your fish market, although you may need to order it in advance. Alternatively, you can order it online from www.icicleseafoods.com.

Jacob's favorite cod roe dip

Serves 6 as an appetizer, or up to 10 as a bite

14 oz [400 g] smoked cod roe, rinsed and membrane removed
4 garlic cloves (unpeeled)
2⅛ cups [500 ml] olive oil
3 slices [100 g] good quality crustless white bread
Scant ½ cup [100 ml] milk
Scant 3 Tbsp [40 g] Dijon mustard
Juice of 2 lemons
Sea salt and freshly ground black pepper
Smoked paprika to sprinkle

To serve
Flatbreads

Put the garlic and olive oil into a saucepan over medium heat and heat until the oil starts to bubble around the garlic cloves. Turn the heat down slightly, so that the garlic doesn't fry, and cook gently for 20 minutes. When the garlic is soft, take the pan off the heat. Leave to infuse and cool completely.

Meanwhile, break the bread into chunks and place in a bowl. Pour on the milk and set aside to soak.

When the oil is cold, remove the garlic cloves with a slotted spoon and peel them; reserve the oil.

Put the cod roe, mustard, lemon juice, and garlic into a blender or food processor. Squeeze the bread to remove excess milk, then add to the blender, and blitz for 1 minute. With the motor running, slowly add most of the garlic oil through the funnel until the mixture thickens and has the consistency of mayonnaise; save some oil for serving.

Season with salt and pepper to taste, and blend for another 20 seconds. Scrape into a bowl, cover, and refrigerate until needed.

When ready to serve, sprinkle the dip generously with smoked paprika, and drizzle with the reserved garlicky olive oil. Accompany with plenty of warm flatbreads.

I particularly like to cook with Mexican flavors in the summer—it just feels right—and this is a great dish to make when tomatoes are at their peak. Sea robin has a lovely sweet flavor, and nice firm texture, which is well suited to deep-frying in this way. Mullet and bass also work well here.

Polenta coated sea robin, corn, red onion, and tomato relish, jalapeño mayonnaise

Serves 4 as an appetizer

2 sea robin, about 21 oz [600 g] each, filleted and pin-boned
¾ cup [100 g] all-purpose flour, for coating
2 large eggs, beaten
1 cup [150 g] fine cornmeal
Sunflower oil for deep-frying
Sea salt and freshly ground black pepper

For the corn, red onion, and tomato relish

6 ripe plum tomatoes
2 ears corn, shucked and silk removed
3 Tbsp olive oil
4 small red onions, diced
2 green chiles, seeded and minced
Juice of 2 limes
2 Tbsp superfine sugar
3 Tbsp chopped cilantro, plus a few sprigs to garnish

For the jalapeño mayonnaise

2 egg yolks
1 Tbsp verjus or white wine vinegar
2 Tbsp jalapeño chiles in vinegar, drained
1 cup [250 ml] sunflower oil
⅓ cup [15 g] flat-leaf parsley, leaves picked and chopped
Scant ⅓ cup [10 g] cilantro, leaves picked and chopped
1 cup [25 g] arugula leaves, chopped
¼ cup [15 g] freshly grated Parmesan

To serve

2 limes, halved

To make the relish, using a small, sharp knife, scoop out the core from each tomato, and score a cross on the bottom of each one. Place in a bowl, pour on boiling water to cover, and leave for 30 seconds. Lift out the tomatoes, peel away the skins, and roughly chop the flesh; set aside.

Cut the corn kernels from the cobs by standing the cobs upright on a board, and cutting downward with a sharp knife.

Heat a large skillet over high heat, and add the olive oil. When hot, add the onions, chiles, and corn. Cook, stirring, over high heat for about 3 minutes, until the onions and corn start to soften and color. Add the chopped tomatoes with a good pinch of salt, and cook for 2 minutes. Remove from the heat, and add the lime juice, sugar, and cilantro. Stir well, then set aside in the pan.

For the mayonnaise, put the egg yolks, verjus, and chiles in a blender or small food processor, and blitz for 30 seconds. Scrape down the sides of the bowl, and blitz again for a few seconds. With the motor running, slowly add half the oil in a thin, steady stream through the funnel. Add the parsley, cilantro, arugula, Parmesan, and a large pinch of salt. Blend for 1 minute. Add the remaining oil in a steady stream, blending until the mayonnaise is thick. Taste and correct the seasoning, then spoon into a bowl, cover, and refrigerate until needed.

Set up three bowls: one with flour, one with beaten eggs, and one with cornmeal. Pass the sea robin fillets through the flour, then the egg, and finally the cornmeal to coat. Place the coated fillets on a plate.

Heat the oil in a deep-fat fryer or other suitable deep, heavy pan to 350°F [180°C]. Deep-fry the fillets in the hot oil, in batches, for about 3 minutes until golden. Remove and drain on paper towels, then sprinkle with salt.

To serve, share the relish between 4 plates. Add a sea robin fillet and a good spoonful of mayonnaise to each plate, and finish with a sprig of cilantro and a lime half.

Appetizers and small bites

If any of your friends or family say they don't like oysters, get them to try these. I've converted no end of staunch avoiders with crispy deep-fried oysters! I wouldn't fry—or even cook—a native Cornish oyster; it's the cheaper and bigger farmed oysters that you want here. Opening oysters might seem a bit daunting at first, but once you have done a few, you'll become more confident.

Fried oyster roll, cucumber and mint relish

Serves 4 as a snack

12 live rock oysters
¾ cup all-purpose flour,
  for coating
2 large eggs, beaten
2⅓ cups [100 g] Japanese
  panko bread crumbs
Sunflower oil for deep-frying
Sea salt and freshly ground
  black pepper

**For the cucumber and
  mint relish**

2 cucumbers
Scant ½ cup [100 ml] cider
  vinegar
¼ cup [50 g] superfine sugar
1 red onion, peeled and finely
  sliced
1 garlic clove, peeled and
  minced
1 tsp fennel seeds
1 green chile, seeded and
  minced
2 Tbsp chopped mint
1 Tbsp chopped flat parsley

To serve

4 white hamburger buns, split
  almost in half
1 bunch of watercress, leaves
  picked

First make the relish. Halve the cucumbers lengthwise, then scoop out the seeds with a teaspoon and discard. Slice the cucumber flesh into half-moon shapes, and place in a bowl. Season with salt, then leave to draw out the excess water for 30 minutes.

Heat the cider vinegar, sugar, red onion, garlic, and fennel seeds in a pan until the sugar has dissolved, then remove from the heat.

Squeeze the cucumber to remove excess water, add to the vinegar mixture, and give it a good stir. Leave to cool completely, then stir in the chopped chile and herbs. Set aside until ready to serve.

Set up three bowls: one with flour, one with beaten eggs and one with bread crumbs. Open the oysters, drain off the juices and check for any fragments of shell. Pass the oysters through the flour, patting off any excess, then through the egg, and finally into the bread crumbs to coat. The oysters can stay in the bread crumbs until you are ready to fry them.

When ready to serve, heat the oil in a deep-fat fryer or other suitable deep, heavy pan to 350°F [180°C].

Toast your hamburger buns and place 2 Tbsp of the relish and some watercress on each base.

Deep-fry the oysters in the hot oil for 1 minute until golden and crisp. Remove, and drain on paper towels. Place 3 crispy oysters on each bun base and close the lid. Serve immediately.

This is my version of the Sicilian classic *arancini*. It's a great recipe and a real crowd pleaser. At my first restaurant, I cooked a lobster risotto flavored with orange, basil, and scallions, which became a signature dish. I've used the same combination here because it works so well.

Lobster risotto balls, basil and orange mayonnaise

Makes about 20; serves 10 as an appetizer

2 live lobsters, about 1¾ lb [800 g] each
4½ cups [1 L] vegetable stock (see page 218)
1½ cups [250 g] carnaroli rice
1 bunch of scallions, trimmed and finely sliced
1½ cups [100 g] Parmesan, freshly grated
Finely grated zest of 1 orange
30 basil leaves, finely sliced
1 large egg, beaten
Heaping 1 cup [150 g] all-purpose flour
4½ cups [500 g] dried bread crumbs
Sunflower oil for deep-frying
Sea salt and freshly ground black pepper

For the basil and orange mayonnaise

2 egg yolks
Finely grated zest of 1 orange
2 Tbsp white wine vinegar
Scant 2 cups [450 ml] light olive oil
4 scallions, trimmed and sliced
20 basil leaves, finely sliced

Put the lobsters in the freezer 30 minutes before cooking to sedate them.

Bring a large pan of well salted water to a boil. To kill the lobsters instantly, place them on a board and insert the tip of a strong, sharp knife firmly into the cross on the back of the head, then plunge the lobsters into the boiling water. Bring back to a boil, and cook for 8 minutes.

Remove the lobsters from the pan to a tray, and leave until cool enough to handle. Twist and pull the claws, legs, and head away from the tails. Put the heads into a pan with the vegetable stock. Crack the claws and extract the meat. Using scissors, cut open the tail shell along its length. Pull the shell apart, and remove the tail meat in one piece. Cut this meat in half lengthwise and remove the dark intestinal tract. Cut the tail and claw meat into small pieces, put into a bowl, cover, and refrigerate.

For the lobster balls, bring the stock (and lobster heads) to a boil. Add the rice with a pinch of salt and bring back to a boil. Reduce the heat, and simmer until the rice has absorbed all the stock. Take off the heat and discard the heads. Stir in the scallions, Parmesan, orange zest, and some pepper. Spread the rice out on a tray, and cool in the fridge.

Meanwhile, for the mayonnaise, put the egg yolks, orange zest, and wine vinegar into a blender or small food processor, and blend for 30 seconds then, with the motor running, slowly add the olive oil in a steady stream. If it gets too thick, add 1 tsp water, then continue. Transfer to a bowl, stir in the scallions, basil, and salt and pepper to taste; set aside.

Once the rice is cold, stir in the sliced basil and lobster meat. Break off pieces and roll into balls, roughly the size of a golf ball. In a bowl, mix the beaten egg and flour together with some salt and pepper until smoothly combined. Place the bread crumbs on a tray. Heat the oil in a deep-fat fryer or other suitable deep, heavy pan to 325°F [160°C].

Pass the lobster balls through the egg mix and then into the bread crumbs, turning to coat all over. Deep-fry in the hot oil, in batches if necessary, for about 2 minutes until crisp and golden. Drain on paper towels and season with salt. Serve hot or cold, with the mayonnaise on the side.

This is a breakfast treat for all seafood lovers. *Bottarga*—the salted, pressed, air-dried roe of either tuna or grey mullet—is considered to be one of the great food delicacies of the world. Of the two, I prefer the more refined, subtle flavor of grey mullet *bottarga*, which is also more sustainable. The keta caviar—salmon roe—is a lovely addition. To give the dish a comforting feel, I sit the poached eggs on creamy horseradish mashed potatoes and liven it up with a grating of fresh horseradish at the end.

Poached eggs with bottarga, salmon roe, and horseradish mash

Serves 4

1 *bottarga*, about 3½ oz [100 g] (you won't need all of it for this recipe)
3½ oz [100 g] keta caviar (ideally wild Alaskan)
8 extra large eggs
3½ Tbsp [50 ml] white wine vinegar

For the horseradish mash
3 large baking potatoes
1 fresh horseradish root, peeled
⅔ cup [150 ml] light cream
Scant ½ cup [100 ml] whole milk
Sea salt and freshly ground black pepper

To serve
1 lemon, cut into 4 wedges

Preheat your oven to 400°F [200°C].

For the mash, bake the potatoes on a baking sheet for 1 hour or until tender. Set aside until cool enough to handle. Meanwhile, grate 3½ Tbsp of the horseradish, and put into a saucepan with the cream and milk. Bring to a simmer, and remove from the heat.

Cut the potatoes in half, scoop out the flesh, and pass through a potato ricer into a bowl, or mash with a potato masher. Fold in the creamy milk to give a soft mash texture. Season with salt and pepper to taste, bearing in mind the *bottarga* and keta are salty. Keep warm.

To poach the eggs, bring a large pan of water to a simmer with the wine vinegar added. Crack each egg into a small individual cup or ramekin, and add to the simmering water. (There is no need to stir the water – if your eggs are fresh they will form a nice shape instantly.) Cook the eggs for 3 minutes.

Meanwhile, lay some paper towels on a plate ready to drain the eggs. When the eggs are cooked, remove them with a slotted spoon, and trim away the escaping bits of egg white if you wish. Drain on the paper towels and season with salt and pepper.

Spoon a portion of horseradish mash onto each of 4 warmed plates, and make a well in the center with the back of the spoon. Place 2 poached eggs in each well, and slice the *bottarga* over the top. Add small spoonfuls of keta, followed by a good grating of horseradish. Serve immediately, with a wedge of lemon.

Believe it or not, this is where it all started for me, with those bright orange crumbed fish bricks from the magic cold place! I'd like to tell you that my love of fish started with bouillabaisse in Provence, or whole turbot cooked over coals in San Sebastian, but no, it was the humble fish finger. Now, of course, I make my own. Eaten burger-style, with lettuce, gherkins and a pea and mint mayonnaise, they are surprisingly good. For a buffet or kids' party, buy smaller rolls and cut smaller fish fingers.

Fish finger roll, pea and mint mayonnaise

Serves 4 as a snack

21 oz [600 g] haddock fillet, skinned, pin-boned, and cut into fingers
¾ cup [100 g] all-purpose flour, for coating
2 large eggs, beaten
Heaping ¾ cup [100 g] dried bread crumbs
Sunflower oil for deep-frying
Sea salt and freshly ground black pepper

For the pea and mint mayonnaise

2 egg yolks
¾ cup [100 g] fresh or frozen peas
1 tsp English mustard
5 tsp malt vinegar
2 Tbsp chopped mint
1¼ cups [300 ml] sunflower oil

To serve

1 iceberg lettuce, finely shredded
2 large gherkins, grated
4 good quality focaccia or other large rolls, split in half
1 lemon, cut into wedges

First make the mayonnaise. Put the egg yolks, peas, mustard, vinegar, and half of the mint into a blender or small food processor, and blend for 30 seconds. Then, with the motor running, add the oil in a slow, steady stream through the funnel until it is fully emulsified. Stop the machine, and add the remaining mint and some salt and pepper, then blend for 30 seconds. Transfer the mayonnaise to a tub, check the seasoning, and refrigerate until needed.

Set up three bowls: one with the flour, one with beaten eggs, and one with bread crumbs. Pass the fish, one piece at a time, though the flour and pat off any excess, then through the egg, and finally through the bread crumbs. Place the breaded fish on a plate. Heat the oil in a deep-fat fryer, or other suitable deep, heavy pan to 350°F [180°C].

Combine the shredded lettuce and grated gherkins with 2 Tbsp of the mayonnaise and mix well, then share equally between the roll bases.

Now fry your fish fingers for 4 minutes until golden and crisp, turning as necessary to color evenly. When the fish is ready, drain on a plate lined with paper towels, and season well with salt.

Lay the hot fish fingers on the rolls and top with a dollop of mayonnaise. Close the lids and serve immediately, with lemon wedges.

Appetizers and small bites

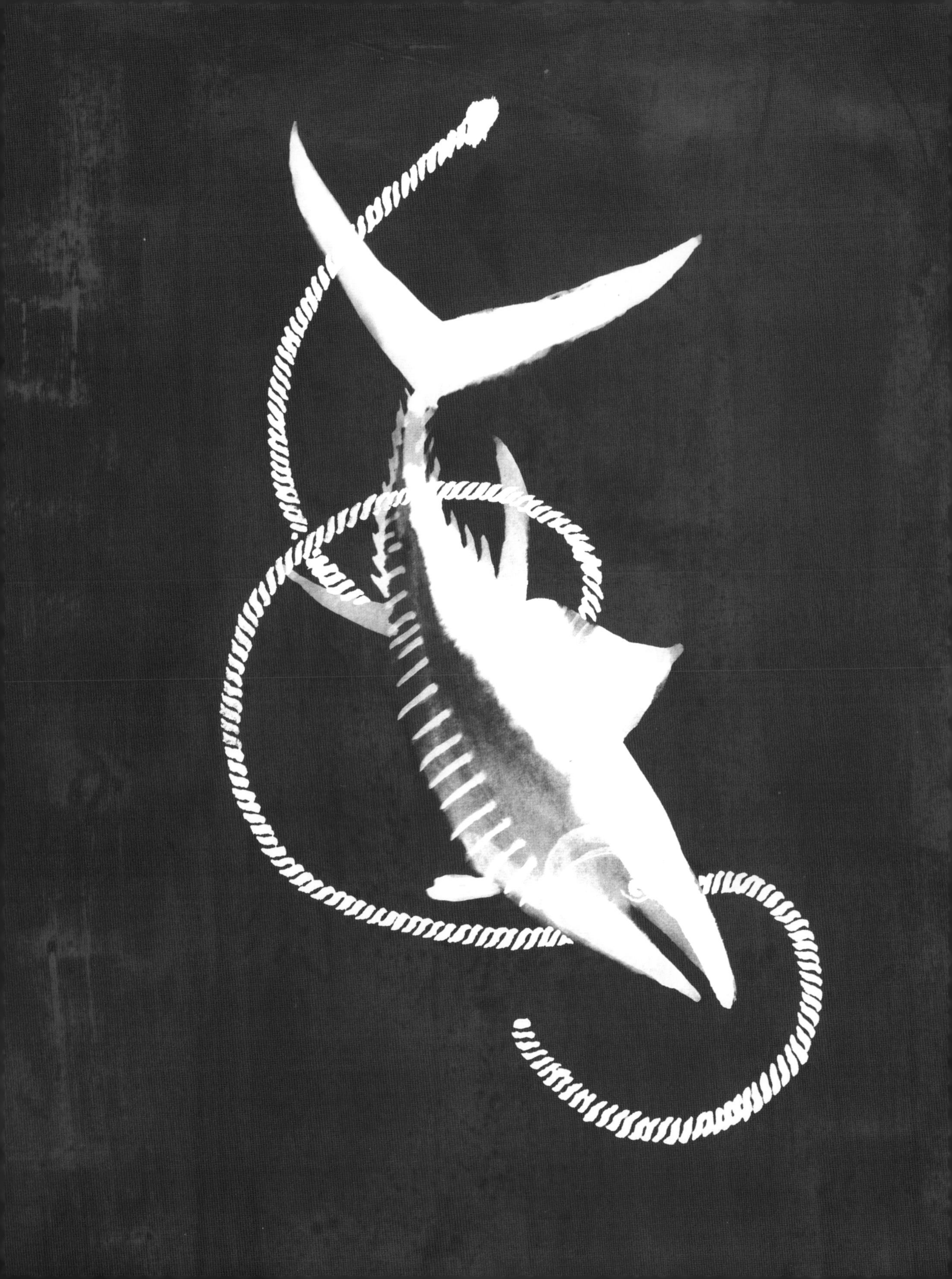

STRAIGHT

FROM

THE SEA

Raw scallops always go down well when we serve them in the restaurants, so I wanted to share a favorite recipe of mine here. Prepare it during the autumn and winter, when celeriac is at its best. I make a stock and a pickle from the celeriac, and finish the dish with celeriac chips, and a drizzle of chili oil.

Raw scallops, celeriac broth, and green chili oil

Serves 4 as an appetizer
12 very fresh scallops, shelled, cleaned, and roes removed

For the celeriac broth
1 large or 2 small celeriac, peeled and diced
2 Tbsp sunflower oil
A good squeeze of lemon juice
Sea salt

For the celeriac pickle
½ celeriac, peeled and cut into matchsticks
⅓ cup [75 ml] hard cider
⅓ cup [75 ml] cider vinegar
⅓ cup [75 ml] water
6 Tbsp superfine sugar
A small handful of cilantro, leaves, picked and chopped

For the celeriac chips
½ celeriac, peeled
Sunflower oil for deep-frying

For the green chili oil
1½ cups [30 g] cilantro, leaves picked
1¼ cups [300 ml] light olive oil
2 green chiles, chopped (seeds left in)

To finish
1 to 2 green chile(s), seeded and minced

First make the chili oil. Add the cilantro to a pan of boiling salted water, and blanch for 30 seconds, then lift out and plunge into a bowl of cold water to refresh. Drain and squeeze out the excess water, then place in a blender. Add the olive oil and chiles, and blitz thoroughly. Pour into a container and place in the fridge for 24 hours. Decant just before serving.

For the broth, weigh the diced celeriac and note the weight. Heat a pan (large enough to hold the celeriac comfortably) and add the olive oil. Add the celeriac and cook over medium heat until caramelized all over, at least 20 minutes. Add the same volume of water as the weight of the celeriac, and bring to a boil. Reduce the heat, and simmer for 20 minutes.

Strain the liquid into a clean pan. (Save the celeriac for a stew or mash with your next meal.) Bring the liquor to a simmer, and let bubble until reduced to about ⅔ cup [150 ml]; it should be a lovely golden brown color. Strain again, and allow to cool. Cover and refrigerate until required.

For the pickle, put the celeriac matchsticks into a bowl. Heat the cider, vinegar, water, sugar, and a pinch of salt in a small pan to dissolve the sugar, and bring to a boil. Pour over the celeriac, cover, and let cool.

For the chips, finely slice the celeriac, using a mandoline, if you have one. Heat the oil in a deep-fat fryer or other suitable deep, heavy pan to 300°F [150°C] Line a tray with paper towels. Fry the celeriac slices in batches, as necessary: lower into the hot oil and fry until golden all over. Remove with a strainer, drain on the paper towels, and sprinkle with sea salt. Allow to cool.

To assemble, drain the pickled celeriac and toss the chopped cilantro through it. On a clean board with a sharp knife, slice the scallops in half horizontally, and season with a little salt.

Share the scallops and celeriac between 4 warmed shallow bowls. Gently warm the broth in a pan, and add salt and lemon juice to taste. Divide equally between the bowls and finish with a drizzle of chili oil and a sprinkling of chiles. Serve immediately, garnished with the celeriac chips.

Straight from the sea

This dish is really quick and fun to make. You can even let your guests do it for themselves if you want! The most important thing is to get hold of some super-fresh salmon. I use organically farmed Loch Duart salmon; for me it works perfectly in the raw and cured salmon dishes I serve.

Raw salmon with vodka, orange, and horseradish

Serves 4 as an appetizer

14 oz [400 g] very fresh
  salmon fillet, skinned
1 orange
1 bunch of scallions, trimmed
  and finely sliced
  on the diagonal
2 Tbsp freshly grated
  horseradish
6 to 8 Tbsp lemon vodka
½ cup [120 ml] olive oil
Sea salt
Tarragon leaves, to finish

Chill 4 flat serving plates in the fridge. Cut away the peel and pith from the orange, then cut out the sections from between the membranes. Cut the orange flesh into small pieces.

Using a very sharp knife and a clean board, slice the salmon thinly (or dice it into small pieces if you find it easier).

Lay the slices of salmon on the chilled plates. Sprinkle with a little salt, then scatter over the scallions, orange, and horseradish.

Mix together the vodka and olive oil and spoon over the salmon equally. Garnish with tarragon leaves, and eat immediately.

Tuna served this way is just fantastic. Taking a beautiful loin of tuna and searing it very quickly in a hot pan, does so much for the flavor, because the inside stays raw and contrasts beautifully with the seared exterior. The sauce is based on a classic salsa verde, with the addition of green olives. It's a great dish for a party because it can be prepared in advance.

Raw tuna with green olive sauce

Serves 4 as an appetizer

21 oz [600 g] very fresh loin
  of tuna (yellowfin)
Light olive oil for cooking
Sea salt and freshly ground
  black pepper

For the green olive sauce

3 scallions, trimmed and
  thinly sliced
1 garlic clove, peeled and
  finely grated
2 Tbsp capers in wine vinegar,
  drained
4 Tbsp pitted green olives
4 good quality tinned anchovy
  fillets in oil, drained
Finely grated zest and juice
  of 1 lemon
A handful of flat-leaf parsley,
  leaves picked
½ handful of mint, leaves
  picked
Scant ½ cup [100 ml] olive oil
20 basil leaves, finely sliced

Season the tuna loin all over with salt and pepper. Have ready a bowl of ice water big enough to hold the tuna loin.

Place a nonstick heavy-bottomed skillet over high heat until the pan is very hot. Lightly oil the tuna and lay it in the hot pan. Sear evenly all over, turning as necessary, then plunge the tuna into the ice water to stop the cooking. Once it is cool, lift out and pat dry with paper towels. Wrap the seared tuna tightly in plastic wrap, and chill in the fridge for at least 30 minutes until ready to serve.

To make the sauce, put the scallions, garlic, capers, olives, and anchovies on a board, sprinkle with the lemon zest, and chop together until the mixture almost turns into a paste. Transfer to a bowl.

Chop the parsley and mint leaves together, add to the sauce and mix well. Add the lemon juice and olive oil, and mix again. Season with salt and pepper to taste. Finally add the sliced basil and fork through. Set aside to allow the flavors to mingle (but not in the fridge).

I like to slice the tuna and lay it out on one large plate to place in the center of the table, but you can plate it individually if you wish. Sprinkle with a little sea salt and serve with the green olive sauce,

Like turbot, brill has a lovely firm texture that makes it ideal for curing and easier to slice once cured than other flat fish varieties. It just takes the salt a bit longer to work its magic though the dense flesh. This is my version of a dish that Pete Biggs, my longstanding head chef, developed at Outlaw's at The Capital Hotel in London. The balance between all the components is lovely. Turbot works equally well here, or try very fresh plaice instead—reducing the curing time by an hour.

Citrus-cured brill with anchovy mayonnaise, basil, and pistachios

Serves 4 as an appetizer

18 oz [500 g] very fresh brill or turbot fillets, skinned and trimmed

For the cure

Scant ½ cup [100 g] sea salt
6½ Tbsp [80 g] superfine sugar
Grated zest of 1 lemon
Grated zest of 1 lime
Grated zest of 1 orange
Scant ½ cup [100 ml] white wine

For the anchovy mayonnaise

2 egg yolks
1 tsp English mustard
4 good quality tinned anchovy fillets in oil, drained
3 Tbsp water
2 Tbsp lemon juice
1¼ cups [300 ml] sunflower oil
Sea salt and freshly ground black pepper

To finish

4 Tbsp pistachio nuts roasted in the shell, shelled and roughly chopped if preferred
8 basil leaves, thinly sliced
Basil oil (see page 216) or olive oil to drizzle

For the cure, put the sea salt, sugar, citrus zests, and white wine into a food processor and blitz for 1 minute. Lay the brill or turbot fillets on a tray, and sprinkle the mixture over them. Turn the fillets over in the cure a few times to ensure they are coated all over. Cover with plastic wrap, and place in the fridge to cure for 3 hours.

To make the mayonnaise, put the egg yolks, mustard, anchovies, water, and lemon juice into a small food processor and blitz for 1 minute. With the motor running, slowly add the oil in a thin, steady stream through the funnel until it is all incorporated. Season with salt and pepper to taste. Transfer to a bowl, cover, and refrigerate until needed.

When the time is up, wash the cure off the brill or turbot fillets with cold water, and pat dry with paper towels. Wrap the fish tightly in plastic wrap, and place back in the fridge for an hour to firm up. (At this stage you can freeze the fish for up to 1 month.)

Using a sharp knife and a clean board, slice the fish thinly, and arrange it equally on 4 plates. Spoon on the mayonnaise, in small blobs, so you have some with each mouthful of fish.

Finish with a sprinkling of chopped pistachios and sliced basil. Finally, drizzle on some basil or olive oil. Serve cold or at room temperature.

Verjus is a natural grape product that we use in various ways in our kitchens. It isn't something you would usually associate with curing fish, but I was determined to give it a try, and after a few attempts, I came up with this recipe. I think the simplicity of this dish is beautiful. The textures of the pumpkin seeds and grapes work so well with the soft cured monkfish.

Verjus-cured monkfish with pumpkin seeds and grape dressing

Serves 4 as an appetizer

21 oz [600 g] very fresh monkfish fillet, skinned and trimmed

For the cure
⅞ cup [200 g] sea salt
½ cup [100 g] superfine sugar
2 Tbsp rosemary leaves
Scant ½ cup [100 ml] verjus

For the grape dressing
2 shallots, peeled and minced
Scant ½ cup [100 ml] verjus
2 tsp Dijon mustard
Scant ½ cup [100 ml] olive oil
10 green seedless grapes, sliced
10 red seedless grapes, sliced
Sea salt

For the garnish
1⅔ cups [400 ml] sunflower oil, for deep-frying
1⅛ cups [150 g] pumpkin seeds
Finely grated zest of 1 lemon
2 tsp finely sliced flat-leaf parsley leaves

For the cure, put the salt, sugar, and rosemary into a food processor and blitz thoroughly.

Lay the monkfish on a tray, and sprinkle evenly with the salt mixture. Turn the fish over a few times to ensure it is coated all over. Drizzle the verjus evenly over the fish, then wrap the whole tray in plastic wrap, and place in the fridge to cure for 3 hours.

When the time is up, unwrap the fish, and wash off the cure with cold water, then pat dry with paper towels. Wrap the fish tightly in fresh plastic wrap, and place back in the fridge for an hour to firm up. (At this stage you can freeze the fish for up to a month.)

To prepare the pumpkin seed garnish, put the oil in a small, deep, heavy pan, add the pumpkin seeds, and heat slowly over medium heat until the seeds begin to puff up. As soon as they start to pop, carefully take the pan off the heat. Using a slotted spoon, remove the seeds from the oil, and drain them on a tray lined with paper towels. Season with salt, and allow to cool.

To make the dressing, put the shallots and verjus into a small pan, bring to a boil, and then transfer the contents of the pan into a bowl. Add the mustard, and whisk to combine. Now add the olive oil in a slow, steady stream, whisking all the time. Season with salt to taste and add the sliced grapes.

Using a sharp knife and a clean board, slice the monkfish as thinly as possible, and arrange it equally on 4 large plates. Spoon the dressing over the fish, sharing the grapes evenly. Scatter over the lemon zest, parsley, and pumpkin seeds, then serve.

Wild sea trout is, for me, a delicacy. I actually prefer it to salmon and find it responds particularly well to curing. Using strong alcohol in the cure helps to achieve a pronounced flavor, and the combination of gin, apple, and fennel works well here. This is a good dish for a party, because it can be prepared in advance, and whipped out of the fridge when you're ready to serve.

Gin-cured sea trout with apple and fennel

Serves 6 as an appetizer

I very fresh side of wild sea trout (steelhead trout), skinned and pin-boned

For the cure

1⅛ cups [250 g] sea salt

1¼ cups [250 g] superfine sugar

2 Tbsp juniper berries, crushed

⅔ cups [150 ml] gin

For the apple and fennel salad

⅞ cup [200 ml] olive oil

2 shallots, peeled and finely sliced

4 juniper berries, finely chopped

Scant ½ cup [100 ml] cider vinegar

2 Tbsp gin

2 fennel bulbs, tough outer layer removed

3 eating apples, such as Braeburn

1 Tbsp finely sliced tarragon

For the cure, put the salt, sugar, and crushed juniper berries into a food processor, and blitz for 3 minutes.

Lay the sea trout on a tray, and sprinkle evenly with the cure mixture. Turn the fish over in the cure a few times to ensure it is coated all over. Drizzle the gin evenly over the fish, then wrap the whole tray in plastic wrap, and place in the fridge to cure for 4 hours.

When the time is up, unwrap the fish and wash off the cure with cold water, then pat dry with paper towels. Wrap the fish tightly in fresh plastic wrap, and place back in the fridge for an hour to firm up. (At this stage you can freeze the fish for up to a month.)

To make the dressing, put the olive oil, shallots, and chopped juniper berries into a small pan over medium heat, until the oil just begins to bubble. Take the pan off the heat, and add the cider vinegar and gin.

Slice the fennel as thinly as possible, using a mandoline if you have one, and place it in a bowl. Peel, core, and grate the apples, then add to the fennel with the tarragon. Toss to combine, and dress the salad with half of the dressing, keeping the rest to finish the dish.

Using a sharp knife and a clean board, slice the trout as thinly as possible and arrange it equally on 4 large plates. Scatter some of the salad over the fish, and drizzle with the remaining dressing; bring to room temperature before serving. Serve the rest of the salad in a bowl on the side.

Eating mackerel raw, straight out of the sea, is something everyone should try. The texture and flavor is unique, indeed I would go so far as saying that flavorwise, mackerel is the best fish to eat raw. Marrying it with apple, celery, and bacon is really successful. This same dish works well with salmon, trout, or scallops.

Raw mackerel with apple, celery, and bacon

Serves 4 as an appetizer

2 very fresh large mackerel, filleted, pin-boned, and skinned
4 slices of smoked bacon
1 eating apple, such as Braeburn
1 shallot, peeled and minced
2 tsp chopped chervil
2 tsp chopped chives
3 Tbsp mayonnaise (see page 219)
Sea salt and freshly ground black pepper

For the pickled celery

3 celery stalks, strings removed (with a peeler)
⅓ cup [75 ml] white wine
⅓ cup [75 ml] white wine vinegar
⅓ cup [75 ml] water
6 Tbsp superfine sugar
1 tsp fennel seeds

To assemble and serve

4 slices of wholegrain or seeded bread, for toasting
A handful of watercress, stalks removed
Cold-pressed canola oil to drizzle
Lemon wedges

First, prepare the pickled celery. Finely slice the celery and set aside. Heat the wine, wine vinegar, water, sugar, and fennel seeds in a pan to dissolve the sugar. Add a pinch of salt, and bring to a boil. Take the pan off the heat and add the celery. Cover with plastic wrap, pushing it down onto the surface to keep the celery fully submerged in the liquor. Leave to cool.

Preheat your broiler to the highest setting. Lay the bacon on the broiler rack, and broil on both sides until crispy. When cool enough to handle, chop the bacon and set aside.

Using a very sharp knife and a clean board, slice the mackerel into ¼ in [5 mm] thick slices. Peel, quarter, and core the apple, then cut into small dice.

Put the mackerel and diced apple into a bowl with the shallot, bacon, and herbs. Toss everything together well, and add the mayonnaise. Mix well again, and taste for seasoning—a grinding of pepper will probably be welcome, but the bacon may well provide enough salt.

To serve, drain the pickled celery. Toast the bread on both sides, and place on the serving plates. Share the mackerel mixture equally between the slices of toast. Scatter the watercress over the plates and put a pile of pickled celery on one side.

Finish with a drizzle of canola oil and serve with lemon wedges.

My head chef, Simon Davies, at Outlaw's Fish Kitchen in Port Isaac, Cornwall, came up with this one. It's a great spring/summer dish. The fish takes on all of the curry flavor, and its texture is transformed. Pickled peppers, coconut yogurt, and fragrant cilantro balance it perfectly. This dish will also work well with bass, bream, and mackerel.

Curry-cured mullet with pickled peppers and coconut yogurt

Serves 4 as an appetizer

18 oz [500 g] very fresh mullet fillet, skinned and pin-boned

For the cure

Scant ¼ cup [50 g] fine sea salt

¼ cup [50 g] superfine sugar

3 Tbsp hot curry powder

For the pickled peppers

1 red bell pepper

1 yellow bell pepper

⅓ cup [75 ml] white wine

⅓ cup [75 ml] white wine vinegar

⅓ cup [75 ml] water

6 Tbsp superfine sugar

1 garlic clove, peeled and crushed

For the coconut yogurt

⅞ cup [200 g] full-fat Greek yogurt

Scant ½ cup [100 ml] thick unsweetened coconut milk

Sea salt

To finish

2 tsp chopped cilantro

Curry oil (see page 216) to drizzle

Micro cilantro cress (optional)

For the cure, mix the salt, sugar, and curry powder together in a bowl. Lay the fish on a tray, and sprinkle evenly with the cure mixture. Turn the fish over in the cure a few times to ensure it is coated all over, then wrap the whole tray in plastic wrap, and place in the fridge to cure for 6 hours.

For the pickled peppers, peel, halve, core, and seed the peppers. Slice the peppers thinly, and place in a bowl. Put the wine, wine vinegar, water, and sugar into a small pan and heat to dissolve the sugar, then bring to a boil. Add the crushed garlic clove, and pour over the peppers. Cover the bowl with plastic wrap, and leave to cool.

For the coconut yogurt, mix the yogurt and coconut milk together in a bowl until evenly combined, and season with salt to taste. Cover and refrigerate until ready to serve.

When the curing time is up, wash the cure off the fish in cold water, and pat dry with paper towels. Wrap the fish tightly in plastic wrap, and return to the fridge for an hour to firm up.

Slice the mullet as thinly as possible, and share between 4 plates. Drain the peppers, and toss them with the cilantro and a drizzle of curry oil. Taste for seasoning, adding a little salt if you like.

Share the peppers between the 4 plates, finishing with spoonfuls of the yogurt, extra curry oil, and cilantro cress, if using.

Salmon has the perfect texture and balance of oiliness for curing. I like to experiment with different cures, and this combination of ale and seaweed is something I came up with for a charity dinner. It's always a challenge to cook fish for large numbers, so I decided not to cook it at all, but cure it instead! Fortunately it went down well. The cucumber and seaweed salad is the ideal complement.

Ale-cured salmon with cucumber and seaweed salad

Serves 4

18 oz [500 g] very fresh wild or organic farmed salmon, trimmed and skinned

For the cure

Scant ½ cup [100 g] sea salt
½ cup [100 g] soft brown sugar
⅔ cup [150 ml] strong ale (I use Sharp's Honey Spice IPA)

For the cucumber and seaweed salad

1 large cucumber
Scant ½ cup [100 ml] olive oil
Scant ⅓ cup [70 ml] light canola oil
3½ Tbsp [50 ml] white wine vinegar
1 large shallot, peeled and minced
2 tsp mixed seaweed flakes
Sea salt

For the salad cream

2 egg yolks
2 tsp dried seaweed
2 tsp English mustard
2 tsp superfine sugar
2 Tbsp lemon juice
Scant ½ cup [100 ml] canola oil
⅔ cup [150 ml] heavy cream

To garnish

1 Tbsp dried seaweed flakes

To cure the salmon, lay the fish on a tray and sprinkle evenly with the salt and sugar. Turn the fish over in the cure a few times to ensure it is coated all over. Drizzle evenly with the ale then wrap the whole tray in plastic wrap and place in the fridge to cure for 6 hours.

For the cucumber salad, put the oils and wine vinegar into a pan with the shallot, seaweed, and a pinch of salt. Bring to a simmer over medium heat, and let bubble for 2 minutes, then remove from the heat and allow to cool.

Meanwhile, halve the cucumber lengthwise, peel, then scoop out and discard the seeds. Thinly slice the cucumber into half-moon shapes. Lay the cucumber slices in a dish, and pour the cooled liquor over them. Cover with plastic wrap, pushing it down onto the surface to keep the cucumber fully submerged. Leave to stand for at least an hour.

To make the salad cream, whisk the egg yolks, seaweed, mustard, sugar, and lemon juice together in a bowl for 1 minute, then gradually whisk in the canola oil, a little at a time, until fully incorporated. To finish, slowly whisk in the cream, and season with salt to taste. Cover and refrigerate until required.

When the salmon curing time is up, unwrap the fish and wash off the cure under cold running water, then pat dry with paper towels. Wrap the fish tightly in fresh plastic wrap and place back in the fridge for an hour to firm up.

To serve, cut the cured salmon into ³⁄₈-in [1 cm] thick slices and divide between 4 plates.

For the dressing, drain off some of the liquor from the cucumber salad into a bowl, and add some of the shallots too. Arrange some of the cucumber salad over the salmon, and spoon on the dressing. Dress the plates with salad cream and seaweed flakes; bring to room temperature before serving. Serve the rest of the salad in a bowl on the side.

This dish has a real kick to it from the ginger and basil, but the mackerel is well up to handling those bold flavors. It would be perfect for a light lunch, or you could easily scale it up for a dinner party. If you have any chutney left over, keep it in the fridge to serve with cheese, cold meats etc. Salmon is a great alternative to the mackerel; just give it an extra 3 hours' curing.

Ginger-cured mackerel, beet chutney

Serves 4

4 large mackerel, heads removed, gutted, filleted, and pin-boned

For the cure
⅞ cup [200 g] sea salt
¾ cup [150 g] superfine sugar
2 tsp black peppercorns
2 tsp coriander seeds
¾ cup [100 g] peeled and grated fresh ginger

For the beet chutney
Scant ½ cup [100 ml] olive oil
1 red onion, peeled and minced
1 garlic clove, peeled and minced
6 Tbsp [50 g] grated fresh ginger
21 oz [600 g] raw beets, peeled and grated
1½ cups [300 g] soft brown sugar
2½ cups [600 ml] cider vinegar
2 bay leaves
4 Granny Smith apples, peeled, cored, and grated
Sea salt and freshly ground black pepper

For the basil and ginger crème fraîche
Heaping ½ cup [75 g] peeled and grated fresh ginger
20 large basil leaves
⅞ cup [200 ml] full-fat crème fraîche

To finish
Cold-pressed canola oil

For the cure, put the salt, sugar, peppercorns, and coriander seeds into a food processor and blitz for 3 minutes. Add the grated ginger, and blitz for another 2 minutes.

Lay the mackerel fillets on a large tray and sprinkle evenly with the cure mixture. Turn the fillets over in the cure a few times to ensure they are coated all over. Wrap the whole tray in plastic wrap, and place in the fridge to cure for 1 hour.

Meanwhile, make the chutney. Heat the olive oil in a large pan over medium heat. When it is hot, add the onion, garlic, and ginger. Sweat for 1 minute, then add the beets and sweat for an additional 2 minutes. Now add the brown sugar and cider vinegar, and bring the mixture to a simmer. Add the bay leaves, and let simmer until the liquid becomes syrupy. Add the grated apples, and cook for 10 minutes, stirring occasionally. Transfer to a bowl, season with salt and pepper to taste. and leave to cool.

For the crème fraîche, put the grated ginger and basil leaves into a blender with the crème fraîche. Blitz for 2 minutes until smooth. Season with salt, and whiz for another 30 seconds. Transfer to a bowl, cover, and refrigerate until ready to serve.

When the fish curing time is up, unwrap the fish and wash off the cure with cold water, then pat dry with paper towels.

Slice the fish as thinly as possible, and arrange it on 4 plates. Spoon the beet chutney into the center, and finish with a drizzle of canola oil. Serve the basil and ginger crème fraîche on the side.

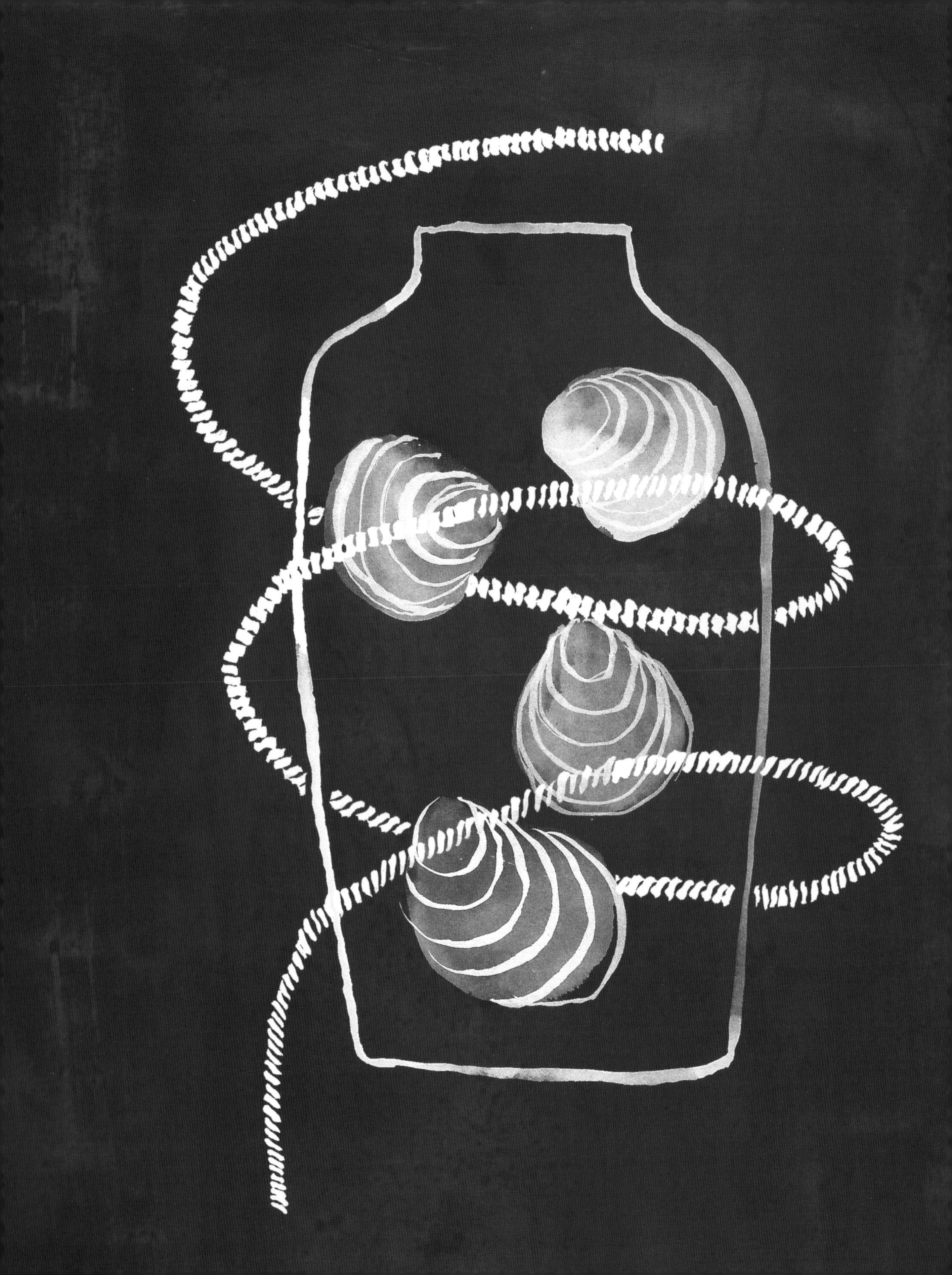

IN A
PICKLE

These oysters are a great party snack. You can get everything done beforehand and just dish them up when you are ready. If you're not mad about raw oysters, then try deep-frying them. Coat the oysters in flour, then beaten egg, and finally with bread crumbs. Fry them in hot oil for a few minutes, drain on paper towels, and serve with the relish on the side.

Cider-pickled oysters with shallot, caper, and apple relish

Serves 4 as an appetizer

12 live Pacific oysters
Scant ½ cup [100 ml] cider vinegar
Scant ½ cup [100 ml] olive oil
2 large banana shallots, peeled and minced
1 red chile, seeded and finely diced
1 Tbsp small capers in brine, drained and rinsed
2 Granny Smith apples
1 Tbsp chopped tarragon
1 Tbsp chopped dill

To serve
Rock salt or seaweed

Open the oysters and strain their juice through a cheesecloth-lined strainer into a measuring cup. Keep the shells.

Pour a scant ½ cup [100 ml] of the oyster juice into a bowl and add the cider vinegar, olive oil, shallots, chile, and capers. Peel and core the apples and cut into fine julienne. Add to the bowl, and mix well.

Now add the oysters and mix gently. Cover with plastic wrap, pushing it down onto the surface to keep the oysters submerged. Leave to pickle for 2 hours.

To serve, clean and dry the oyster shells thoroughly. Place the shells on a bed of seaweed or salt to hold them steady.

Remove the oysters from the bowl, and place one in each shell. Stir the chopped herbs through the relish. Top the oysters with a generous spoonful of the relish, and serve immediately.

When I opened my Fish Kitchen in Port Isaac, Cornwall, we put this dish on the menu and it went down a storm. The pickled vegetables are a relatively recent addition—I think they bring the whole thing alive. Conveniently, I share a pub in Rock with Sharp's Brewery (who brew Doom Bar amber ale), called The Mariners, and this dish now sits happily on the menu there.

Doom Bar marinated seafood

Serves 8 as an appetizer

1 octopus (double sucker species), about 2¼ lb [1 kg], defrosted if frozen
2¼ lb [1 kg] live mussels
2¼ lb [1 kg] live cockles
18 oz [500 g] raw shrimp, heads removed, peeled and deveined
2⅛ cups [500 ml] Sharp's Doom Bar amber ale, or similar ale
3 bay leaves
4 thyme sprigs
2 garlic cloves, peeled, halved, and germ removed
3½ oz [100 g] marinated anchovy fillets
Scant ½ cup [100 ml] cold-pressed canola oil
Freshly ground black pepper

For the pickled vegetables

1 cup [250 ml] white wine vinegar
1 cup [250 ml] water
1¼ cups [250 g] soft brown sugar
2 banana shallots, peeled and sliced
1 fennel bulb, outer layer removed, thinly sliced (ideally on a mandoline)
2 carrots, pared and sliced into julienne (ideally on a mandoline)
Sea salt

Put the octopus into a pan with the ale, bay, thyme, and garlic. Pour on enough water to cover, and bring to a boil over medium heat. Skim off any impurities, reduce the heat, and simmer for 1 hour until tender.

Meanwhile, prepare the pickled vegetables. Put the wine vinegar, water, and sugar into a pan and heat to dissolve the sugar. Bring to a simmer, season with salt, and simmer for 2 minutes. Put the shallots, fennel, and carrots into a bowl, and pour on the hot pickling liquor. Cover with plastic wrap, pushing it down onto the surface to keep the vegetables submerged.

To cook the mussels and cockles, place a large saucepan (with a tight-fitting lid) over high heat. When hot, add the mussels, cockles, and a ladleful of the octopus stock. Cover, and cook for 2 minutes. Check if the shells are open. If not, put the lid back on and continue to cook, checking every 30 seconds, until all or most are open.

Tip the contents of the pan into a colander set over a bowl to catch the juices. Discard any unopened molluscs. When cool enough to handle, pick the meat out of the shells. Pour the juices through a cheesecloth-lined strainer into the octopus pan. Refrigerate the mussels and cockles.

Lift the cooked octopus out of the pan; strain and reserve the liquor. Cut the tentacles from the body. Slit open the body and remove the ink sac, stomach, and eyes. Slice the tentacles and body meat into 1¼ to 1½ in [3 to 4 cm] pieces.

Strain off the liquor from the veg into a pan, and add the same volume of octopus stock. Bring to a boil, skim if necessary, then add the shrimp, and immediately take off the heat. After 2 minutes, remove the shrimp with a slotted spoon; set aside to cool with the octopus. Cool the liquor.

Add the mussels, cockles, octopus, shrimp, anchovies, and vegetables to the cooled liquor. Mix well, then leave to marinate and pickle overnight.

To serve, drain the seafood and vegetables, reserving the liquor. Season with pepper to taste. Lay on a large platter. Mix ⅞ cup [200 ml] of the pickling liquor with the canola oil and use to dress the salad.

Every time I buy razor clams, I smile as I think of the very first person who ate them—they must have been adventurous, and very hungry. If you've ever seen a live razor clam, you will understand what I mean. Thank goodness they are so tasty! Here, I lightly pickle the razors and serve them with a crunchy carrot and fennel chutney and a spicy and cooling yogurt... delicious.

Razor clams, carrot and fennel chutney, jalapeño yogurt

Serves 4 as an appetizer

20 live razor clams
Sea salt

For the pickling liquor

⅓ cup [75 ml] cider vinegar
⅓ cup [75 ml] hard cider
⅓ cup [75 ml] water
¼ cup [50 g] superfine sugar

For the carrot and fennel chutney

1 fennel bulb, tough outer layer removed
2 carrots, pared
1 shallot, peeled and finely sliced
1 red chile, seeded and finely sliced
3½ Tbsp [50 ml] cider vinegar
¼ cup [50 g] superfine sugar
1 tsp fennel seeds
1 tsp black onion seeds
2 Tbsp finely sliced cilantro
1 Tbsp finely sliced mint, plus extra to finish

For the jalapeño yogurt

⅞ cup [200 g] full-fat Greek yogurt
3 tsp chopped jalapeño chiles in vinegar, drained
2 tsp chopped mint

Set up a steamer. Lay the razor clams on a tray and steam for 2 minutes until they open. Carefully remove the razors from the steamer, and save their juices. Allow to cool slightly, then remove from their shells. Prepare the razors by cutting away the dark and sandy parts, reserving the white, creamy pieces. Clean the 12 best shells and set aside for use later.

For the pickling liquor, put all the ingredients into a pan, and heat to dissolve the sugar, then bring to a simmer and simmer for 2 minutes. Add a pinch of salt, remove from the heat, and leave to cool.

When the pickling liquor is cold, add the razor clams, cover, and place in the fridge to pickle for at least 30 minutes.

For the chutney, finely slice the fennel, using a mandoline if you have one. Grate the carrots, or cut into very fine julienne, and place in a bowl with the fennel. Put the shallot and chile into a small pan with the cider vinegar, sugar, fennel seeds, and onion seeds Heat to dissolve the sugar, then bring to a simmer and pour the mixture over the carrot and fennel. Mix well, and season with salt to taste. Finally, stir through the cilantro and mint.

For the yogurt, in a bowl, mix the yogurt with the chopped jalapeños and mint. Season with salt to taste, then cover and chill until required.

To serve, mix the razor clam meat and chutney together. Spoon into the cleaned shells and place three on each serving plate. Spoon some of the jalapeño yogurt onto each shell and sprinkle with a little extra mint. Serve immediately.

It doesn't get much simpler than this Peruvian-style dish. It's such a great, healthy way to eat seafood, and makes a lovely appetizer for a dinner party. All you need is really fresh fish. Here I've used bass, but I've also made it successfully with salmon, mackerel, brill, and scallops. Just be sure to taste it as you go: it's important to get the balance of the heat from the chiles, the acidity from the lime, and the level of saltiness right.

A simple bass ceviche

Serves 4 as an appetizer
14 oz [400 g] very fresh bass
  fillet, skinned, pin-boned,
  and trimmed
1 small red onion, peeled and
  minced
2 green chiles, seeded and
  minced
12 good quality baby plum
  tomatoes, halved lengthwise
Finely grated zest of 1 lime
Juice of 2 limes
A handful of cilantro, leaves
  picked and chopped
2 ripe avocados
Sea salt

To serve
⅞ cup [200 g] sour cream
Olive oil to drizzle
1 lime, cut into wedges

Cut the bass into dice and place in a bowl with the red onion, chiles, tomatoes, lime zest, and juice. Season with salt, and add the chopped cilantro. Toss well to mix, then cover, and leave to cure in the fridge for 10 minutes.

Just before serving, halve, peel, and pit the avocados, then cut into dice, the same size as the bass pieces. Toss the avocado through the bass mixture. Taste for seasoning, and add more salt if needed.

Divide the ceviche between 4 plates. Top with a dollop of sour cream, and add a drizzle of olive oil to each plate. Serve with lime wedges.

Mullet is really tasty, so it's a shame it has acquired a bad reputation, owing to its liking for brackish and stagnant waters. Your fish market should be able to reassure you that his or her fish has been caught in clean water. The oiliness of the flesh partly accounts for its excellent flavor; it also works well in a dish like this. Based on a ceviche, citrus juice cooks the fish, and turns it into something fantastic. If you can't get mullet, use bass or bream instead.

Mullet with fennel, lime, and orange

Serves 4 as an appetizer

18 oz [500 g] very fresh mullet fillet, pin-boned and skinned
1 Tbsp olive oil, plus extra to finish
2 red onions, peeled and sliced
2 red chiles, halved, seeded and sliced
2 garlic cloves, peeled and minced
2 oranges
Juice of 2 limes
2 fennel bulbs, tough outer layer removed
4 radishes, trimmed
2 Tbsp cilantro leaves, finely sliced
Sea salt

Place a small pan over medium heat, and add the olive oil. When it is hot, add one of the sliced onions and sweat for 2 minutes. Next, add the chiles and garlic, and sweat for an additional 2 minutes. Transfer to a blender, and blitz well to a paste. Allow this chili paste to cool.

Soak the other sliced onion in cold water to cover for 5 minutes. Drain, then dry on paper towels. Put the onion into a bowl, cover and place in the fridge until needed.

Slice the fish thinly, season with salt, and place in a bowl. Leave to stand for 5 minutes.

Meanwhile, squeeze the juice from one of the oranges. Cut away the peel and pith from the other orange, and cut out the sections from between the membranes; cut these into smaller pieces.

Drizzle the orange and lime juices over the fish, and mix well. Cover with plastic wrap, and place in the fridge for 20 minutes. During this time the fish will effectively "cook" in the citrus juice.

In the meantime, slice the fennel very thinly, ideally on a mandoline, then place it in a bowl of cold water to firm and crisp up. Do the same with the radishes.

When the fish is ready, drain off the juice, then add 1 Tbsp chili paste and toss to mix. Drain the fennel and radishes and add them to the fish along with the orange pieces, red onion slices, and sliced cilantro. Toss to combine, and taste for seasoning, adding more salt if needed.

To serve, divide between individual plates or shallow bowls, and drizzle with a little olive oil.

When mackerel is around, I can't get enough of it and I always try to find new ways of serving it. Once autumn arrives, mackerel is plentiful, as are cabbages and apples, so it makes sense to bring them together. Here, crunchy red cabbage and crisp apple complement soft, rich mackerel, and the cider tones from the salad cream and pickle, marry them together perfectly.

Pickled mackerel with red cabbage, apple, and cider

Serves 4

4 very fresh mackerel, filleted and pin-boned
1 Tbsp olive oil
1 red onion, peeled and thinly sliced
½ red cabbage, outer leaves removed, thinly sliced
2 Braeburn apples, peeled and grated
Sea salt

For the pickling liquor

⅞ cup [200 ml] cider vinegar
⅞ cup [200 ml] hard cider
¼ cup [50 g] superfine sugar
1 garlic clove, peeled and crushed
2 thyme sprigs
2 bay leaves

For the salad cream

2 egg yolks
1 tsp English mustard
2 tsp superfine sugar
2 Tbsp cider vinegar
2 Tbsp hard cider
Scant 1½ cups [350 ml] olive oil
3½ Tbsp heavy cream
2 Tbsp dill leaves, chopped, plus extra sprigs to garnish

For the pickling liquor, put all the ingredients into a pan, and heat to dissolve the sugar, then bring to a boil, reduce the heat, and simmer for 2 minutes. Add a pinch of salt.

Lay the mackerel fillets side by side in a dish that holds them snugly in one layer. Pour on the pickling liquor, and cover with plastic wrap, pushing it down onto the surface to keep everything submerged. Leave to stand for 2 hours: the fish will effectively "cook" in the liquor. (It can be kept in the liquor for up to 2 days.)

Meanwhile, heat a small skillet, and add the olive oil. When the oil is hot, add the red onion and sweat for 2 to 3 minutes. Season with salt, and transfer the onion to a tray to cool.

To make the salad cream, put the egg yolks, mustard, sugar, cider vinegar, and hard cider into a bowl, and whisk together for 1 minute. Now gradually add the olive oil, drop by drop to begin with, then in a thin, steady stream until it is all incorporated. To finish, slowly whisk in the cream, and season with salt to taste. Transfer to a bowl, and stir through the chopped dill. Cover and refrigerate until required.

To serve, combine the onion, red cabbage, and apples in a bowl. Mix well, and season with salt to taste.

Remove the mackerel fillets from the pickle. Spoon some salad cream onto each of 4 plates, and pile the red cabbage mixture into the center. Arrange the mackerel fillets on top. Add a sprinkle of sea salt, and finish with a few dill sprigs.

We go herring mad when they come into season in Cornwall, and prepare them in all sorts of ways. Pickling is one of my favorite treatments, and this recipe is incredibly simple. Just make sure your herring are top quality, and really fresh. Feel free to change the flavorings, if you like, and don't worry about the small bones—they disintegrate in the pickling mix.

Pickled herring, orange, red onion, and tarragon dressing

Serves 4 as an appetizer

8 very fresh herring, gutted, scaled, and filleted
3 shallots, peeled and finely sliced
3 garlic cloves, peeled and crushed
1 tsp dried red pepper flakes
4 tsp fennel seeds
2 bay leaves
2⅛ cups [500 ml] white wine vinegar
1 cup [200 g] superfine sugar
3 oranges
⅞ cup [200 ml] orange oil (see page 216)
2 red onions, peeled, halved, and thinly sliced
4 Tbsp tarragon leaves, chopped
Sea salt

Lay the herring fillets side by side in a dish that is big enough to hold them snugly, covered by the pickling liquor.

Put the shallots, garlic, red pepper flakes, fennel seeds, and bay leaves into a pan. Add the wine vinegar, sugar, and the finely grated zest of one of the oranges. Bring to a simmer, and simmer for 2 minutes, then add 4 tsp salt. Remove from the heat, and allow to cool.

Once cooled, pour the pickling mix over the herring fillets, and cover with plastic wrap, pushing it down onto the surface to keep the fish submerged. Place in the fridge, and leave for 24 hours before eating.

Take the fish out of the fridge at least an hour before serving to bring it back to room temperature. Cut the peel and pith from all 3 oranges, and cut out the sections from between the membranes.

For the dressing, measure 3½ Tbsp of the pickling liquor, and mix it with the orange oil, orange sections, red onion slices, and chopped tarragon. Season with salt to taste.

Lay the herring fillets on a large platter, and spoon over the orange, red onion and tarragon dressing. Serve with sourdough and salted butter.

In a pickle

Sea robin has a lovely meaty quality, and a unique flavor that I love. It can handle big flavors too, including my red pepper ketchup. This dish will sit quite happily in the fridge for up to 3 days. Just make sure you take it out of the fridge a few hours before serving to bring the flavors alive.

Soused sea robin, red pepper ketchup, arugula and black olive salad

Serves 4 as a main course

4 very fresh small sea robin, about 21 oz [600 g] each, or 2 larger fish, filleted and pin-boned
1 cup [250 ml] olive oil
2 onions, peeled and sliced
2 red bell peppers, cored, seeded and sliced
$^1/_3$ cup [75 ml] red wine vinegar
2 garlic cloves, peeled and sliced
2 rosemary sprigs
A handful of flat-leaf parsley, leaves picked and chopped
Sea salt

For the red pepper ketchup

3½ Tbsp [50 ml] olive oil
2 red onions, peeled and chopped
3 red bell peppers, peeled, cored, seeded, and chopped
2 garlic cloves, peeled and sliced
1 red chile, seeded and chopped
18 oz [500 g] ripe tomatoes, chopped
6 Tbsp superfine sugar
1 rosemary sprig, leaves picked and chopped
Scant ½ cup [100 ml] white wine vinegar
Scant ½ cup [100 ml] balsamic vinegar
2 oz [55 g] tin good quality anchovy fillets in oil, drained

For the arugula and olive salad

2 handfuls of arugula leaves
Scant 1 cup [100 g] black olives, pitted
Finely grated zest and juice of 1 lemon
A drizzle of olive oil

Heat a large nonstick skillet and add a drizzle of olive oil. When hot, add the sea robin fillets, and fry until the skin side is golden. Turn the fillets over in the pan, count to 30, and then remove to an oven dish.

Add a little more oil to the skillet, then add the onions and peppers and sweat for 4 to 5 minutes, until the peppers soften and start to collapse. Add the remaining olive oil, wine vinegar, garlic, and rosemary and bring to a simmer. Season with salt, and pour over the fish fillets. Cover with plastic wrap, pushing it down onto the surface to keep the fish submerged. Leave to souse for at least 2 hours.

To make the ketchup, place a large pan over medium heat, and add the olive oil. When hot, add the onions, peppers, garlic and red chile, and cook for 4 minutes until the onions are translucent. Add the tomatoes with the sugar and rosemary, and cook for 15 minutes until they have broken down. Add both vinegars and the anchovies, and let bubble until the liquor becomes syrupy.

Transfer the mixture to a blender or food processor, and blitz until smooth, then pass through a strainer into a bowl. Taste for seasoning, and adjust with salt to taste. Cover and leave to cool. (The ketchup will keep fine in a sealed container in the fridge for up to a week; it can also be frozen.)

For the salad, toss the arugula, olives, and lemon zest together and dress with lemon juice, olive oil, and salt to taste. Arrange on 4 plates.

Lift the sea robin out of the sousing liquid, and share the fillets between the plates. Pass the sousing liquid through a strainer into a bowl. Transfer the peppers from the strainer to another bowl, add the chopped parsley, and mix well. Divide the peppers between the plates.

Finish with a drizzle of sousing liquid and a generous spoonful of the red pepper ketchup.

I like to cook English sole on the bone, so the fillets keep their natural shape. If you fillet the fish first, the fillets tend to shrink quite a lot during cooking. Sousing English sole is unusual, but I find the acidity is welcome, and it adds more depth of flavor. The mushrooms and seaweed marry well with the vinegar and wine, but nothing outshines the star of the show, the English sole.

Hot soused English sole with mushroom and seaweed dressing

Serves 4 as a main course

4 English sole, about 18 oz [500 g] each, skinned and heads removed

Scant ½ cup [100 ml] olive oil

2 red onions, peeled and sliced

10½ oz [300 g] mixed mushrooms, cleaned

4 garlic cloves, peeled and minced

Scant ½ cup [100 ml] sherry vinegar

Scant ½ cup [100 ml] white wine

2 Tbsp dried seaweed flakes

2 Tbsp chopped flat-leaf parsley

Sea salt and freshly ground black pepper

Preheat your oven to 400°F [200°C].

Heat a large skillet and add a drizzle of olive oil. When hot, add the red onions, and cook for 3 to 4 minutes until they start to soften. Scatter the onions in a roasting pan big enough to hold the fish (or use 2 or 4 smaller pans).

Wipe out the skillet and heat again. When hot, add another drizzle of oil. Toss in the mushrooms and cook for 3 minutes, then add the garlic, and continue to cook for another 2 minutes. Season with salt and pepper and add to the onions in the pan(s).

Wipe out the skillet again. Season the fish all over with salt and pepper. Heat the skillet and add a drizzle of olive oil. When hot, add the English soles and fry for 2 minutes. Turn the fish over, and cook for an additional 2 minutes.

Mix the sherry vinegar and wine together, and add to the pan to deglaze. Remove from the heat and add the seaweed and any remaining olive oil. Transfer the fish to the pan(s), spooning some of the mushrooms and onions on top of them, then pour over the juices from the skillet. Bake for 8 to 10 minutes until cooked.

Sprinkle the chopped parsley over the cooked fish, then carefully transfer to warmed plates. Spoon the mushrooms, onions, and juices over the fish. I like to serve this simply with boiled new potatoes and seasonal green vegetables.

The most common hot marinated dish is the classic escabeche, which I adore. The technique works well with lots of fish—you just need to get the balance of acidity and heat right. As lemon sole fillets are thin, they are well suited, because they readily take on the acidity of the marinade and "cook" quickly. This is a great dish for two, but you can easily double or triple the quantities to serve more.

Hot marinated lemon sole with pickled onions and grapes

Serves 2 as a main course

2 lemon soles, about 18 oz [500 g] each, scaled and filleted

For the pickling marinade
Olive oil for cooking
12 pearl onions, peeled and left whole
2 celery stalks, strings removed (with a peeler) and finely sliced
2 garlic cloves, halved and germ removed, minced
1 green chile, halved, seeded, and minced
1 rosemary sprig, leaves picked and minced
14 oz [400 g] canned cannellini or other white beans, drained
⅓ cup [75 ml] verjus
Scant ½ cup [100 ml] white wine
1 cup [250 ml] fish stock (see page 218)
Sea salt and freshly ground black pepper

To assemble and serve
1 Tbsp chopped chives
1 Tbsp chopped flat-leaf parsley
20 red seedless grapes, halved
A drizzle of extra virgin olive oil

To prepare the pickling marinade, heat a large saucepan over medium heat, and add a generous drizzle of olive oil. When the oil is hot, add the pearl onions and cook for 4 to 5 minutes, turning occasionally to color evenly.

When the onions are nice and golden, add the celery, garlic, chile, and rosemary, and cook for 2 minutes. Add the white beans to the pan, and cook for another 2 minutes, then add the verjus, and cook for an additional 2 minutes. Pour in the wine and stock, bring to a boil, and season with salt and pepper. Remove from the heat.

Lay the lemon sole fillets in a dish large enough to hold the fish flat and level. Bring the marinade back to a simmer, then carefully pour it over the fish. Leave to stand for 10 minutes.

Just before serving, scatter the chives, parsley, and grapes over the fish, and finish with a drizzle of olive oil over the top.

BOWL
FOOD

When asparagus is at its best in the UK, so are the prized male "cock" crabs and it makes perfect sense to pair these two delicacies. The result is magic, and one of my all-time favorites. I finish this simple dish with a drizzle of emerald green seaweed oil, which I make from the gutweed we gather around the beaches close to the restaurants. If you find it hard to get hold of, make a parsley or chive oil following the same method instead.

Chilled asparagus soup, crabmeat, and seaweed oil

Serves 4 as an appetizer

9 oz [250 g] white crabmeat (from a 3¼ lb [1.5 kg] freshly cooked crab)
Olive oil for cooking and serving
2 shallots, peeled and finely sliced
1 potato, peeled and thinly sliced
4½ cups [1 L] vegetable stock (see page 218)
21 oz [600 g] asparagus, woody parts removed, thinly sliced
1¼ cups [300 ml] heavy cream
A squeeze of lemon juice
Sea salt and freshly ground black pepper

For the seaweed oil

2 large handfuls of gutweed, thoroughly washed and picked
A large handful of spinach leaves
2 cups [500 ml] sunflower oil

To prepare the seaweed oil, bring a pan of water to a boil, add the seaweed and spinach, and blanch for 30 seconds. Remove and plunge into a bowl of ice water to cool. Drain thoroughly, and squeeze out all excess water. Transfer to a blender, add the oil, and blend thoroughly. Transfer to a bowl or pitcher, cover and refrigerate until needed.

To make the soup, heat a large saucepan over medium heat, and add a drizzle of olive oil. When hot, add the shallots and potato, and cook for 2 minutes. Pour in the stock, bring to a boil, then reduce the heat and simmer for 10 minutes until the potato is cooked.

Add the asparagus, and cook for 1 minute. Meanwhile, set a bowl (large enough to hold the soup) over another bowl filled with ice.

Pour the cream into the soup, bring back to a boil, and season with salt and pepper to taste. Transfer to a blender, let cool slightly, then blitz until smooth. Pour the soup into the bowl (over ice) to cool it quickly.

When the soup is cold, cover and place in the fridge until ready to serve. Chill 4 soup bowls too.

When ready to serve, check the white crabmeat for any fragments of shell or cartilage. Divide most of the crabmeat between the chilled soup bowls, holding a little back for the garnish. Season the crabmeat, and add a drizzle of olive oil and a squeeze of lemon juice.

Give the soup a good stir and check the seasoning again. Share the soup equally between the bowls, and top each one with some crabmeat. Finish with a drizzle of seaweed oil.

One of the best memories I have of Singapore is the food markets and stalls. I love the fact that you can sit in the market and try all the different foods that are on offer. The shrimp noodle soup I tasted there was something else. I wasn't quite sure how they made it, but after a few trials I think this is pretty close... it tastes good anyway.

Shrimp noodle soup

Serves 4 as an appetizer

For the stock

18 oz [500 g] raw Atlantic shrimp in the shell, plus extra shells and heads (see below)

A generous drizzle of sunflower oil

4 garlic cloves, peeled and sliced

4½ cups [1 L] water

For the soup

1 Tbsp sunflower oil

7 oz [200 g] piece of smoked bacon, cut into lardons (diced)

4 scallions, trimmed, white and green parts separated and sliced

2 red chiles, seeded and thinly sliced

2 garlic cloves, peeled and minced

5 Tbsp fish sauce

2 Tbsp white wine

10½ oz [300 g] rice noodles

16 raw tiger shrimp, shelled and deveined (keep shells and heads for stock)

2 bok choy, sliced into strips

1¼ cups [70 g] beansprouts

Sea salt and freshly ground black pepper

To make the shrimp stock, heat the oil in a sauté pan, then add the garlic, and cook until golden. Add the shrimp (plus the extra shells and heads from the shelled shrimp for the soup) and cook until they turn orangey-red all over. Crush the shrimp with the back of a spoon, then add the water, and bring to a boil. Add a good pinch of salt, and simmer for 25 minutes. Strain through a strainer into a bowl and set aside.

To make the soup, heat the oil in a large saucepan. When it is hot, add the bacon, white scallions, chiles, and garlic. Sweat for 5 minutes, stirring every so often.

Now pour in the shrimp stock, bring to a simmer, and cook gently for 10 minutes. Stir in the fish sauce and wine. Season with salt and pepper to taste.

Add the rice noodles to the pan, and cook for 3 minutes. Add the shrimp and bok choy, and cook for an additional 2 minutes until they turn orangey-red. Finally, add the green scallions and bean sprouts.

To serve, ladle the soup into 4 warmed bowls, dividing the noodles, beansprouts, bok choy, and shrimp evenly. Serve immediately.

This is a brilliant soup to make in late summer when fresh corn is at its best. It proved a real crowd pleaser when I served little bowls of it in the restaurant as a pre-dinner *amuse bouche*. Beautiful seared scallops complement the corn flavor perfectly, while the pickled red onions cut the richness and stop the soup becoming too sweet.

Corn soup with scallops and pickled red onions

Serves 4 as an appetizer or light lunch

12 fresh scallops, shelled and cleaned (roes retained if in good condition)
4 ears corn, shucked and silk removed
Olive oil for cooking and to drizzle
5 Tbsp unsalted butter
4 tsp chopped cilantro leaves
Sea salt and freshly ground black pepper

For the pickled red onions
2 small red onions, peeled and finely sliced into rings
Scant ½ cup [100 ml] red wine
Scant ½ cup [100 ml] red wine vinegar
½ cup [100 g] superfine sugar
Scant ½ cup [100 ml] water

Cut the corn kernels from the cobs, by standing the cobs upright on a board and cutting downward with a sharp knife.

Heat a drizzle of olive oil and the butter in a large saucepan over medium heat, then add the corn. Cook for 15 to 20 minutes, stirring every couple of minutes so the corn toasts at the edges, but does not burn. Pour in enough water to barely cover it, and bring to a simmer. Cook for about 15 minutes, until the corn is tender.

Meanwhile, prepare the pickled onions. Put the red onion slices into a bowl. Heat the wine, wine vinegar, sugar, and water in a small pan to dissolve the sugar, then bring to a boil. Add a pinch of salt, and pour this pickling liquor over the onion slices. Cover, and leave to cool.

When the corn is tender, blitz with the cooking liquor in a blender, or using a stick blender in the pan, for 3 to 4 minutes until smooth. Return to the pan, and taste for seasoning, adding salt and pepper as you like. If the soup is too thick, add a little more water. Leave over low heat while you cook the scallops.

Heat a large nonstick skillet over medium heat, and add a drizzle of olive oil. Season the scallops with salt, and place, one by one, in the hot pan, remembering where you placed the first one. Cook for 2 minutes until golden, then carefully flip them over in the same order you placed them in the pan. Take off the heat, and allow the scallops to finish cooking in the residual heat.

Drain the pickled onions (you can save the pickling liquor to use again).

Bring the soup back to a simmer, and divide between 4 warmed bowls. Place 3 scallops in each bowl and add some pickled red onion slices and a scattering of chopped cilantro. Finish with a drizzle of olive oil, and serve immediately.

I make lots of different chowders, especially in winter, as I love the hearty and warming feeling it gives you when you eat one. This is a favorite: the salty clams and almost crunchy texture of the shrimp are great with the rich broth. I like to add plenty of fresh herbs, and a splash of verjus at the end to lift the flavors. Feel free to change any of the ingredients, but stick to the technique—it works so well.

Clam and shrimp chowder

Serves 4 as an appetizer or light lunch

16 raw shrimp, shelled and heads removed (keep for cooking) and deveined
2 large handfuls of live surf, Venus, carpet shell, or other live clams available to you
3⅓ cups [800 ml] whole milk
⅞ cup [200 ml] heavy cream
2 garlic cloves, peeled, halved (germ removed) and minced
10½ oz [300 g] potatoes, such as Yukon Gold, peeled and thinly sliced
½ cup [125 ml] verjus
3½ Tbsp cold-pressed canola oil, plus extra to drizzle
2 large banana shallots or 6 ordinary shallots, peeled and minced
1 leek, outer layer removed, halved lengthwise, washed well and finely sliced
2 celery stalks, strings removed (with a peeler) and cut into 1cm dice
1 small celeriac, peeled and cut into ⅜ in [1 cm] dice
1 red chile, halved, seeded, and finely sliced
Scant ½ cup [100 ml] dry hard cider
2⅛ cups [500 ml] fish stock
½ handful of dill, leaves picked and minced
½ handful of tarragon, leaves picked and minced
Sea salt and freshly ground black pepper

To make the chowder, pour the milk and cream into a large pan, and add the garlic and potatoes. Tie the shrimp heads and shells in cheesecloth, and add to the pan. Bring to a simmer and simmer for 10 minutes, or until the potatoes are soft.

Meanwhile, heat another large pan with a tight-fitting lid over high heat. When hot, add the clams and a scant ½ cup [100 ml] verjus. Immediately put the lid on, and steam for 3 minutes until the shells open. Pour the contents of the pan into a colander set over a bowl, to catch the juices. Set aside.

Wipe the pan clean, and place over medium heat. When it is hot, add the canola oil, followed by the shallots, leek, celery, celeriac, and chile. Cook, stirring occasionally, for 5 minutes without coloring. Now pour in the cider and fish stock, and bring to a simmer. Cook for 10 minutes, until the vegetables are softened.

In the meantime, remove and discard the cheesecloth bag of shrimp shells from the chowder pan, then transfer the contents of the pan to a blender, and blitz until smooth. Add to the vegetables and stock, along with the reserved clam juice. Stir and check the seasoning, adding salt and pepper to taste.

Pick three-quarters of the clams out of their shells, leaving the rest in. Bring the chowder to a simmer. Add the shrimp, and cook for 2 minutes, until they turn pink, then add all the clams, herbs, and the remaining splash of verjus.

Turn off the heat, and stir the chowder gently to avoid breaking the clam shells. Ladle into a warmed tureen or soup bowls, and drizzle some canola oil over the surface. Serve immediately.

This Japanese-style broth may not be authentic, but I can whip it up in minutes at home and it tastes so good. The combination of red mullet (goatfish) and East Asian mushrooms is amazing. If not available, you can make this with bream or sea bass You should be able to buy dashi flakes quite easily, but shiso might be a little more difficult to find. Shiso is like a Japanese basil, so you could use basil in its place. If you don't have time to make the shiso oil, add a splash of toasted sesame oil instead.

Red mullet and mushroom miso broth with shiso oil

Serves 4 as a hearty appetizer or light lunch

2 red mullet (goatfish), bream, or sea bass, about 18 oz [500 g] each, scaled, filleted and pin-boned

3½ Tbsp light canola oil, plus extra for oiling

4½ cups [1 L] water

1 Tbsp instant dashi flakes

2 Tbsp white miso paste

2 cups [50 g] dried porcini mushrooms

6 scallions, finely sliced (white and green parts separated)

1 cluster [50 g] shimeji mushrooms

½ cup [50 g] eryngii (or oyster)mushrooms

1 cup [75 g] shiitake mushrooms

1 garlic clove, peeled and minced

Juice of 1 lime

10½ oz [300 g] dried udon noodles

7 oz [200 g] tofu, cut into cubes

Sea salt and freshly ground black pepper

For the shiso oil

2 handfuls of shiso leaves

2 large handfuls spinach leaves

Heaping ⅓ cup [50 g] fresh ginger, peeled and shredded

2 tsp superfine sugar

⅞ cup [200 ml] light canola oil

First make the shiso oil. Have a bowl of ice water ready. Bring a pan of salted water to a boil, add the shiso and spinach leaves, and cook for 1 minute. Remove immediately, and plunge into the ice water to cool quickly. Drain and squeeze out the excess water.

Put the shiso and spinach into a blender and add the ginger, sugar, canola oil, and some salt and pepper. Blitz for 2 minutes, then pour into a pitcher or bowl, cover, and refrigerate.

Preheat your broiler to high. Oil a broiler pan and sprinkle with salt and pepper. Slice each red mullet fillet into 2 equal pieces, lay on the broiler pan and turn to coat in the oil and seasoning, then place skin side up. Set aside.

Put the water and dashi flakes into a saucepan over medium heat, and bring to a simmer, then whisk in the miso paste and dried porcini. Cover the pan, remove from the heat, and leave to stand for 10 minutes.

Meanwhile, heat a skillet over medium heat, and add the canola oil. When hot, add the white scallions and all of the mushrooms. Cook for 3 minutes, then add the garlic. Season with salt and pepper to taste, and add the lime juice, stirring to deglaze. Remove from the heat, and set aside.

Strain the miso liquor through a fine strainer into a clean pan, discarding the porcini, and bring to a boil. Add the noodles and cook for 2 minutes until they are just tender.

Cook the fish under the broiler for 2 minutes. Add the green scallions and tofu to the broth, and heat for 1 minute.

Ladle the broth, noodles, and mushrooms into 4 warmed bowls, sharing them equally. Add 2 pieces of red mullet to each bowl and finish with a drizzle of shiso oil. Serve immediately.

Smoked haddock makes such a lovely, comforting soup. It marries perfectly with egg and bacon in this hearty chowder for a nourishing lunch or supper, or even brunch, if you fancy. It's worth buying really good quality smoked haddock—avoid that cheap, bright yellow dyed stuff.

Smoked haddock soup with poached egg and pancetta

Serves 4 as a hearty appetizer or light lunch

21 oz [600 g] smoked haddock fillet, skinned, pin-boned, and diced (trimmings saved)
⅞ cup [200 ml] fish stock (see page 218)
⅞ cup [200 ml] milk
Scant ½ cup [100 ml] heavy cream
Olive oil for cooking and to drizzle
2 white onions, peeled and minced
1 celery stalk, strings removed (with a peeler) and thinly sliced
2 garlic cloves, peeled and minced
1 large potato, peeled and diced
6 thin slices of pancetta
Scant ½ cup [100 ml] white wine vinegar
4 extra large eggs
Sea salt and freshly ground black pepper

Pour the fish stock, milk, and cream into a saucepan, and add the smoked haddock trimmings. Bring to a boil, and then take off the heat.

Place another large saucepan over medium heat, and add a little olive oil. When hot, add the onions, celery, and garlic. Cook, stirring occasionally, for 4 minutes, then stir in the diced potato. Strain the creamy milk and stock mixture over the vegetables, and bring to a simmer. Cook gently for 8 to 10 minutes until the potatoes are soft. Let cool slightly, then transfer to a blender, and blitz until smooth.

Meanwhile, preheat your broiler to high, and lay the pancetta on a broiler pan. Bring a large pan of water to a simmer with the wine vinegar added.

Place the pancetta under the broiler, and cook until crispy. Carefully crack the eggs into the simmering water. (There is no need to stir the water— if your eggs are fresh, they will form a nice shape instantly.) Poach the eggs for 3 minutes.

Meanwhile, add the smoked haddock to the soup, and cook gently for 2 minutes. Remove from the heat, and taste for seasoning, adding salt and pepper if you wish.

Cut the broiled pancetta in half. When the poached eggs are ready, drain them on paper towels.

Share the soup equally between 4 warmed bowls. Place a poached egg in each bowl, season with pepper, and surround with the crispy pancetta. Add a generous drizzle of olive oil and serve immediately.

If you enjoy fragrant Thai flavors, you will love this dish. The classic Thai aromatics really help to bring the flavors of the seafood alive. I've used razor clams and queenie scallops, but shrimp or any other shellfish will work. The chili oil is a nice finishing touch if you like a bit of heat.

Razor clam and scallop soup with coconut, lemongrass, and chile

Serves 4 as a hearty appetizer or light lunch

4½ lb [2 kg] live razor clams
20 queenie scallops, cleaned, or 8 standard sea scallops, cleaned and halved
3½ Tbsp [50 ml] sunflower oil
2 red onions, peeled and finely sliced
3 lemongrass stalks, tough outer layers removed, minced
Scant ½ cup [50 g] fresh ginger, peeled and finely grated
2 garlic cloves, peeled and minced
2 bird's eye chiles, seeded and minced
3¼ cups [800 ml] canned coconut milk
2 Tbsp fish sauce
3 Tbsp lime juice
A handful of cilantro, leaves picked
2 handfuls of baby spinach leaves
Chili oil (see page 216) to finish

Check that your clams are alive and closed; discard any that are open. Place a large pan with a tight-fitting lid over high heat. When hot, add the clams with a mugful of water. Immediately put the lid on, and steam the clams for 2 minutes until the shells open. Pour the contents of the pan into a colander set over a bowl, to catch the juices. Leave to cool.

Wipe the pan clean, and place over medium heat. When hot, add the oil, followed by the onions, lemongrass, ginger, garlic, and chiles. Cook, stirring, for 2 minutes, then pour in the coconut milk, and bring to a simmer. Allow to simmer for 5 minutes.

Meanwhile, prepare the clams. Remove the meat from the shells, then cut away and discard the sandy and black parts. Slice the meat into even-sized pieces, and set aside. Pass the clam juice through a fine strainer into a bowl and reserve.

Add the fish sauce, lime juice, cilantro, spinach, and strained clam juice to the coconut liquor, and bring back to a boil. Stir in the scallops, and return to a simmer. Remove from the heat, and stir in the razor clam meat; the scallops will finish cooking in the residual heat.

Ladle the soup equally into 4 warmed bowls. Drizzle with a little chili oil, and serve with crusty bread.

I often make this quick and healthy soup at home—even the kids like it! The smoky oiliness of mackerel is great with fresh tasting parsley and spinach, and the horseradish adds a lovely kick. You can vary the leafy green veg and/or herb if you like. If you want to make the soup in advance, chill it down quickly in a bowl over ice to retain that lovely green color and fresh flavor.

Parsley soup, smoked mackerel, horseradish and lemon oil

Serves 4 as a lunch

6 smoked mackerel fillets
3½ Tbsp light olive oil, plus extra to drizzle
3½ Tbsp unsalted butter
2 banana shallots, peeled and minced
3 garlic cloves, peeled, halved (germ removed) and minced
2 large Yukon Gold potatoes, peeled, and finely sliced
6¼ cups [1.5 L] fish or vegetable stock (see page 218)
2 Tbsp creamed horseradish
3 handfuls of flat-leaf parsley, leaves picked
2 large handfuls of baby spinach leaves
Sea salt and freshly ground black pepper
Horseradish and lemon oil (see page 216), to finish

Cut each smoked mackerel fillet into 3 pieces.

Heat a large saucepan over medium heat, and add the 3½ Tbsp olive oil with the butter. When hot, add the shallots and garlic, and cook for 2 minutes until translucent. Now add the potatoes with some salt and pepper. Cook, stirring constantly, for 2 minutes.

Pour in the stock, bring to a simmer, and cook until the potato is soft, about 8 to 10 minutes. If you don't cook it enough, the soup will have a grainy texture. Pour the contents of the pan into a blender, and add the creamed horseradish.

Wipe the pan clean, return to the heat and add a drizzle of olive oil. When hot, add the parsley and spinach, and cook until wilted.

Transfer the parsley and spinach to the blender, and blend until smooth (see note). Return the soup to the pan, heat until piping hot, then taste and adjust the seasoning if necessary.

Divide the soup equally between 4 warmed bowls and top with the pieces of smoked mackerel. Finish with a drizzle of horseradish and lemon oil.

Note Be very careful when blending a hot soup, as hot air builds up in the pitcher, and will burst out of the top if it is not released. I suggest you pulse it slowly at first with a cloth over the top, then as the soup begins to blend down, blitz in the usual way.

When I opened Outlaw's Fish Kitchen in Port Isaac, I wanted to do a new mussel dish that screamed out "Cornwall!" and showed off our fantastic mussels. This is that dish: a marriage of cider, apple, sage, and clotted cream. Flavors that to me work wonders with the plumpest and juiciest mussels. A simple, quick dish that really impresses every time I cook it.

Mussels with sage, cider, and clotted cream

Serves 2 as an appetizer or light lunch

2¼ lb [1 kg] live mussels
A drizzle of cold-pressed canola oil
2 small white onions, peeled and sliced
8 sage leaves, finely sliced
Scant ½ cup [100 g] Cornish clotted cream, or very heavy cream
⅞ cup [200 ml] medium-dry hard cider
1 Braeburn apple, peeled, cored, and diced
2 Tbsp chopped flat-leaf parsley
Freshly ground black pepper

Wash the mussels, and pull away the hairy beard attached to one end of the shell. Discard any mussels that are open and refuse to close when pinched back together, and any that have damaged shells.

Place a large pan that has a tight-fitting lid over high heat. When it is hot, add the oil, followed by the onions. Cook, stirring frequently, for 3 minutes, until they soften and singe at the edge.

Add the mussels, sage, and clotted cream, cover, and cook for 30 seconds. Lift the lid, pour in the cider and re-cover. Cook for 3 minutes. Lift the lid to check if the mussels are open. If not, put the lid back on and cook for an additional 30 seconds, or until all, or most of the mussels are open.

Add the diced apple and chopped parsley, and toss to mix. Divide the mussels between 2 warmed bowls and pour over the tasty liquor. Serve immediately, with crusty bread and butter.

This dish is very popular when it goes on any of our menus. The scallops we get are hand-dived off the south coast of Cornwall and have a unique texture and taste. Our supply is dependent on the weather, so we treasure them as a luxury ingredient. Their incomparable sweet flavor and beautiful texture really shine through in this simple dish.

Pan-fried scallops, creamed Belgian endive, orange and tarragon dressing

Serves 4 as an appetizer or light lunch

16 to 20 fresh scallops, shelled and cleaned (roes retained if in good condition)
Olive oil for cooking
Sea salt and freshly ground black pepper

For the Belgian endive

2 Belgian endive heads, outer leaves removed, shredded
Scant 1½ cups [350 ml] olive oil
⅓ cup [75 g] unsalted butter
2½ Tbsp superfine sugar
1 white onion, peeled and finely sliced
Finely grated zest and juice of ½ orange
⅔ cup [150 ml] heavy cream

For the orange and tarragon dressing

1 orange
½ cup [120 ml] extra virgin olive oil

To finish

1 Tbsp chopped tarragon

For the Belgian endive, heat a large skillet over medium-high heat and add the olive oil, butter, and sugar. When hot, add the onion and cook, stirring occasionally, for 2 minutes. Now add the Belgian endive, and cook for 2 minutes, turning from time to time.

Turn the heat down under the Belgian endive to medium, and add the orange zest and juice. Let the juice bubble away, then add the cream. Bring to a simmer, and let simmer for 5 minutes. Remove from the heat.

Meanwhile, for the dressing, cut the peel and pith from the orange, and cut out the sections from the membranes over a bowl to catch any juice. Slice the orange sections, and place in a bowl with the extra virgin olive oil, and some salt and pepper. Set aside.

To cook the scallops, heat a nonstick pan until very hot. Season the scallops with salt, and drizzle some olive oil into the pan. Carefully place the scallops in the pan, one by one, remembering where you placed the first one. Turn the heat down to medium and cook for 2 minutes. Now flip the scallops over in the same order you placed them in the pan, and cook for an additional minute. Take the pan off the heat, and allow the scallops to finish cooking in the residual heat.

To serve, warm up the creamed Belgian endive if need be, then taste and correct the seasoning. Divide the Belgian endive between 4 warmed plates or shallow bowls, and top each serving with 4 or 5 scallops. Add a good drizzle of orange dressing, and sprinkle with the chopped tarragon. Serve warm.

On a trip to Singapore I became a little obsessed with crab dishes, and set about re-creating the exciting street food I had eaten. The crabs we have in the UK and US are different to those in Asia, which are smaller and have softer shells. Still, it's easy enough to flavor our crab in the same way, and cook it in a similar fashion. You need plenty of bread and beer with this scrumptious spicy dish.

Crab with tomatoes, chile, green peppercorns, and herbs

Serves 6

3 live Dungeness or blue crabs, about 3½ lb [1.5 kg] each

For the sauce
Scant ½ cup [100 ml] olive oil
3 white onions, peeled and chopped
2 bunches of scallions, cut into fine julienne, white and green parts separated
6 garlic cloves, peeled and minced
2 green chiles, sliced (seeds left in)
14 ripe plum tomatoes, chopped
⅔ cup [150 ml] verjus
2½ cups [600 ml] white wine
2 Tbsp green peppercorns
2 Tbsp chopped tarragon
2 Tbsp chopped chives
3 Tbsp chopped parsley
Sea salt and freshly ground black pepper

To make the sauce, heat the olive oil in a large skillet over medium heat. When hot, add the onions, white scallions, garlic, and chiles, and cook for 4 to 5 minutes until the onions are soft and starting to color. Add the tomatoes and cook, stirring occasionally, for 4 to 5 minutes.

Add the verjus and cook for an additional 5 minutes, then pour in the wine and let it bubble to reduce down. Add the green peppercorns, and season with salt and pepper to taste. Simmer for another couple of minutes, then remove from the heat and set aside.

To cook the crabs, bring a very large pan of very salty water (2 Tbsp salt to 4½ cups [1 L] water) to a boil. When it is almost boiling, lay each crab on its back on a board. Lift the flap near the bottom, and plunge a large chef's knife into the point underneath to kill the crab instantly. Immediately plunge the crabs into boiling water, and cook for 12 minutes.

Lift the cooked crabs out onto a large tray, and leave until cool enough to handle. Hold the crab in both hands and use your thumbs to push the body up and out of the hard top shell. Twist off the claws and legs, and crack them. Remove and discard the dead man's fingers, stomach sac, and hard membranes from the body shell. Now, cut the body in half, and then into quarters.

To finish the dish, heat the sauce, and add the green scallions and chopped herbs. When the sauce comes to a simmer, taste for seasoning, and adjust as necessary. Add all of the crab, give it a gentle stir, and warm through for a couple of minutes.

To serve, carefully transfer the contents of the pan to a large warmed serving dish. Place in the center of the table with finger bowls, spoons, beer, and bread.

This risotto is versatile. I love the pairing of cockles and seaweed, but you could use any seafood in place of the cockles, or even a mixture of seafood if you wish. Similarly, any good seaweed will work, even crushed nori sheets that you buy for sushi—it just needs to be dehydrated and blitzed, to tenderize in the risotto. Adding the hot stock little by little, and stirring continuously helps to release the starch from the rice grains, giving you that wonderful, creamy end result. Have all the ingredients prepared before you start, so you can concentrate on the stirring.

Cockle and seaweed risotto

Serves 4

2¼ lb [1kg] live cockles
5 slices [150 g] wholegrain or sourdough bread, crusts removed and torn into pieces
3½ Tbsp light olive oil, plus extra to drizzle
4½ cups [1 L] vegetable or fish stock (see page 218)
3½ Tbsp unsalted butter
1 large white onion, peeled and minced
1 fennel bulb, tough outer layer removed, minced
2 garlic cloves, peeled, halved (germ removed) and minced
Scant 1½ cups [240 g] carnaroli risotto rice
3½ Tbsp white wine vinegar
Scant ½ cup [100 ml] dry white wine
2 Tbsp dried seaweed flakes, plus an extra 1 tsp to garnish
1¼ cups [100 g] freshly grated Parmesan cheese
8 scallions, trimmed and thinly sliced
A handful of tarragon, leaves picked and chopped
A handful of dill, leaves picked and minced
Grated zest of 1 lime
Sea salt and freshly ground black pepper

Preheat your oven to 400°F [200°C]. Put the pieces of bread on an oven pan, drizzle with olive oil, and season with salt and pepper. Bake in the oven for 10 minutes until golden and crispy.

Meanwhile, bring the stock to a simmer in a saucepan over low heat, and keep it at a steady simmer.

Place another large heavy-bottomed saucepan over medium heat, and add the olive oil and butter. When the butter starts to bubble, add the onion, fennel, and garlic, and cook for 3 minutes, until the onion is translucent. Add the rice, and cook, stirring, for 2 minutes.

Transfer the crisp bread pieces to a plate lined with paper towels to drain; set aside.

Pour the wine vinegar and wine into the rice pan, and cook, stirring, until reduced right down to almost nothing, about 3 minutes. Add the 2 Tbsp dried seaweed. Now add the stock, a ladleful at a time, and cook, stirring slowly and continuously with a wooden spoon, for 12 minutes. Allow each ladleful of stock to be fully absorbed before you add the next.

Next add the cockles along with another ladleful of stock and cook for 2 minutes, or until the cockles start to open. Immediately add the grated Parmesan, scallions, and chopped herbs, and turn off the heat.

Give the risotto a careful stir, and share between 4 warmed plates. Scatter over the crisp bread pieces and lime zest, and finish with a sprinkling of seaweed. Serve immediately.

Fish stew exists all around the globe. Where you are, or where you live, determines what goes in. I like to use fish with a firm texture that will give a real depth of flavor. Roasting the fish heads and bones—and cooking the vegetables in the way I do here—really intensifies the flavors. The scallops are a nice touch of luxury; along with the mussels, they add their own unique quality.

My fish stew

Serves 8

1 monkfish tail, about 3½ lb [1.5 kg], bone removed and reserved, trimmed of sinews
2 sea robin, 21 oz [600 g] each, filleted (heads and bones reserved)
8 large or 16 medium scallops, shelled and cleaned
40 live mussels, bearded and rinsed (see page 99)
1 garlic clove, peeled and chopped
1 rosemary sprig, leaves picked and chopped
Zest of 1 lemon (microplaned)
Scant ½ cup [100 ml] light olive oil
1 large cod head, cleaned
1¼ cups [300 ml] white wine
Sea salt and freshly ground black pepper

For the stew

2 onions, peeled and sliced
4 garlic cloves, peeled and crushed
2 fennel bulbs, minced
2 red bell peppers, cored, seeded, and sliced
½ tsp dried red pepper flakes
Zest and juice of ½ orange (zest microplaned)
A big pinch of saffron strands
3 bay leaves
1 rosemary sprig
3½ Tbsp [50 g] tomato paste
8 ripe tomatoes, chopped

To serve

1 large baguette
Light canola oil for frying
1 garlic clove, halved
Spicy anchovy mayonnaise (see page 219)

Preheat your oven to 350°F [180°C].

Cut the monkfish into 8 equal chunks. Halve each sea robin fillet to give 8 pieces. Put the monkfish, sea robin, scallops, and mussels into a bowl and add the garlic, rosemary, lemon zest, olive oil, and some salt and pepper. Mix carefully, cover, and leave to marinate in the fridge for 1 hour.

To make the stock, line a roasting pan with a sheet of baking parchment. Lay the cod head and reserved fish heads and bones on the paper and roast for 25 minutes. Turn them over and roast for another 25 minutes.

Place the pan over medium heat on the stove. Add the wine, stirring and scraping to deglaze. Simmer for 5 minutes, then transfer everything to a big cooking pot, and add water to cover. Bring to a boil, and skim off any impurities from the surface. Reduce the heat, and simmer for 30 minutes.

Meanwhile, heat another large pan over medium heat, and add a drizzle of olive oil. When it is hot, add the onions, garlic, fennel. and red peppers. Cook, stirring occasionally, for 5 minutes. Now add the red pepper flakes, orange zest, saffron, bay, and rosemary, and cook for 2 minutes. Add the tomato paste, and cook, stirring frequently, for 5 minutes.

Add the chopped tomatoes and orange juice. Cook, stirring occasionally, for 10 minutes. Pour the stock through a strainer onto the vegetables and simmer for 20 minutes. Taste and adjust the seasoning, if necessary.

In the meantime, cut the baguette into thin slices. Heat a ⅜ in [1 cm] depth of canola oil in a wide pan. When hot, shallow-fry the bread slices until golden on both sides. Drain the croûtes on paper towels, rub with the cut surface of the garlic, and season with salt.

Add the monkfish to the stew base and cook for 1 minute, then add the sea robin, and mussels, and cook for another 2 minutes. Finally add the scallops and cook for 1 minute.

Serve the stew in the center of the table with the croûtes and spicy anchovy mayonnaise on the side.

This stew is very simple and quick to cook. It's a recipe that has saved me a few times when I've been really up against it. I've used beans here, but potatoes also work well. You can include seasonal vegetables too, if you like—I often add squash in the autumn and asparagus during spring. Monkfish is great for this sort of dish, because it can handle bold flavors, and it doesn't break up on cooking. If you can't get hold of monkfish, try using sea robin, mullet or shrimp— they all work well.

Monkfish, bean, and bacon stew

Serves 4

21 oz [600 g] monkfish fillet, trimmed, and cut into equal chunks
A drizzle of olive oil
3½ Tbsp unsalted butter
2 red onions, peeled and chopped
2 garlic cloves, peeled and chopped
4¼ oz [120 g] piece of smoked bacon, cut into lardons (diced)
14 oz [400 g] canned cannellini beans, drained
1 Tbsp thyme leaves
4½ cups [1 L] fish or vegetable stock (see page 218)
A handful of flat-leaf parsley, chopped
Sea salt and freshly ground black pepper

Heat a large pan over medium heat, and add the olive oil and butter. When hot, add the onions and garlic, and cook until the onions begin to color. Add the bacon, and cook for 5 minutes, stirring from time to time to make sure it colors evenly. No burnt bits!

Add the cannellini beans, thyme, and stock, and simmer for 20 minutes. Now add the monkfish, and poach gently for 4 minutes. Season with salt to taste.

To finish, add the chopped parsley, and stir gently. Share the stew equally between 4 warmed bowls, and serve some green vegetables on the side, if you wish, and hunks of good crusty bread.

Squid is perfect for a curry, because it readily takes on the spicing and responds well to slow cooking; this is especially true of bigger squid. If you can't get hold of squid, or simply want a quicker curry, you can use a firm fleshed fish like monkfish, or sea robin instead. I've used curry powder here for convenience, but you can grind and mix your own spices if you prefer.

Squid curry with chickpeas and spinach

Serves 4

1¼ to 1¾ lb [600 to 800 g] squid, cleaned, and cut into equal chunks
Sunflower oil for cooking
2 white onions, peeled and chopped
4 garlic cloves, peeled and chopped
2 Tbsp chopped fresh ginger
2 red chiles, seeded and chopped
2 tsp Madras curry powder
1 tsp garam masala
1 eggplant, peeled and diced
21 oz [600 g] ripe tomatoes, chopped
14 oz [400 ml] canned coconut milk
14 oz [400 g] canned chickpeas, drained
2 large handfuls baby spinach leaves
A handful of cilantro, leaves picked
Sea salt

Heat a large sauté pan over high heat, then add a drizzle of oil. When hot, add the squid chunks, and fry for 3 minutes, turning as necessary to color evenly. Transfer the squid to a colander set over a bowl.

Place the pan back over medium heat, and add another drizzle of oil. When hot, add the onions, garlic, ginger, and chiles. Fry for 5 minutes, until the onions are softened, and starting to brown. Stir in the curry powder and garam masala, and cook for another 2 minutes.

Now add the eggplant and tomatoes, and cook for another 5 minutes until the vegetables begin to collapse. Give the curry base a really good stir, and then return the squid to the pan. Pour in the coconut milk, and top up with enough water to just cover everything. Bring to a boil, and add a good pinch of salt.

Turn the heat down so that the curry is simmering very gently, and cook for 1½ hours, topping up the liquor with more water if necessary, to ensure everything remains covered.

When the squid is soft and cooked, add the chickpeas and cook for an additional 15 minutes, but don't add any more water now—you want the liquor to reduce and thicken.

Add the spinach and cilantro, then taste for seasoning, adding more salt if required.

Share the curry equally between 4 warmed bowls, and serve with yogurt and rice if you like. I prefer to eat it on its own with naan bread to mop up the sauce.

Bowl food

This recipe is dedicated to Joseph Tyers, a truly gifted chef, who is sadly no longer with us. Joe's parents found it in the collection of recipes he wrote, and told me it was one of his favorites. I didn't have the opportunity to taste the kedgeree cooked by Joe, but I've since made it several times and it's always well received. So this is Joe's recipe, not mine. I hope you enjoy it... we all have.

Joe's kedgeree

Serves 4

14 oz [400 g] smoked
  haddock, skinned
Heaping 1½ cups [300 g]
  long-grain rice
4 large or extra large eggs
A splash of sunflower oil
3½ Tbsp unsalted butter
2 shallots, peeled and minced
1 leek (white part only), well
  washed and finely sliced
1 celery stalk (strings removed
  (with a peeler) and finely
  sliced
1 garlic clove, peeled and
  minced
A pinch of saffron strands
½ tsp curry powder
3 cups [700 ml] fish stock
  (see page 218)
2 tsp chopped cilantro leaves
Sea salt and freshly ground
  black pepper
1 lemon, cut into wedges,
  to serve

Preheat your oven to 400°F [200°C]. Check the smoked haddock for any pin bones, and cut it into ¾-in [2 cm] squares; set aside.

Wash the rice in cold water 4 or 5 times, changing the water each time. Drain, and allow to stand in the colander for 15 minutes.

Add the eggs to a pan of simmering salted water, return to a simmer, and cook for 8 to 10 minutes. Drain, and briefly run under cold water to cool, then peel and slice.

Place a large ovenproof sauté pan over medium heat, and add the oil and butter. When hot, add the shallots, leek, celery, and garlic, and cook for 2 minutes without coloring.

Add the rice to the pan, stir, and cook for 1 minute. Now add the saffron and curry powder, and stir well over the heat.

Pour in the fish stock, and bring to a simmer. Put the lid on, and place the pan in the oven for 15 minutes, or until the rice is cooked.

Remove from the oven, stir through the pieces of smoked haddock, and immediately put the lid back on. Leave to stand for 3 to 5 minutes; the fish will cook in the residual heat.

Remove the lid, and carefully fold through the sliced boiled eggs and cilantro. Season with salt and pepper to taste. Serve the kedgeree in warmed bowls, with lemon wedges on the side.

This is a really heart-warming winter bowl of food. Ox cheeks have a great flavor, and become meltingly tender if you cook them right. Here they make a brilliant partner for meaty cod cheeks. Both can handle ale quite well, so the marriage is a happy (cheeky!) one. Monkfish cheeks work equally well here, if you happen to come across them. I like to serve this with a rutabaga, carrot, and horseradish mash.

Cod and ox cheek stew

Serves 4

18 oz [500 g] cod cheeks, trimmed of sinews
2 ox cheeks, trimmed of sinews
⅔ cup [75 ml] olive oil
2 Tbsp all-purpose flour
3½ oz [100 g] piece of smoked bacon, cut into lardons (diced)
4 shallots, peeled and chopped
6 garlic cloves, peeled and chopped
2 rosemary sprigs, leaves picked and chopped
4 Tbsp tomato paste
6 ripe plum tomatoes, chopped
Scant ½ cup [100 ml] red wine vinegar
2⅛ cups [500 ml] Sharp's Doom Bar amber ale, or similar ale
4 carrots, pared and halved lengthwise
4 tsp chopped parsley
Grated zest of 1 lemon
Sea salt and freshly ground black pepper

Preheat your oven to 275°F [135°C].

To cook the ox cheeks, heat a heavy-bottomed ovenproof sauté pan over medium-high heat, then add 3 Tbsp of the olive oil. Dust the ox cheeks with the flour, seasoned with salt and pepper. Add the ox cheeks to the pan, and fry for 4 minutes, turning as necessary to color evenly all over. Using a slotted spoon, remove the ox cheeks to a plate.

Add the remaining olive oil to the pan, followed by the bacon, shallots, garlic, and rosemary. Sweat over medium heat for 3 to 4 minutes, then add the tomato paste, and cook for an additional 4 minutes. Add the chopped tomatoes, and cook for another 5 minutes, stirring occasionally.

Return the ox cheeks to the pan, and add the wine vinegar and ale. Bring to a simmer, then top up the liquor with enough water to cover the ox cheeks. Bring back to a simmer, put the lid on, and transfer the pan to the oven. Cook slowly for 4 hours. To check that the ox cheeks are done, lift the lid and pierce one with a knife; it should pass through easily. If there is some resistance, they will need a bit longer in the oven.

In the meantime, steam or boil the carrots until just tender.

Once the ox cheeks are cooked, transfer the pan back to the stove. Add the cod cheeks to the stew, along with the carrots. Return to a simmer and poach gently for 3 to 4 minutes.

To serve, share the stew equally between 4 warmed bowls. Finish with a sprinkling of chopped parsley and grated lemon zest. Serve with mashed root vegetables, flavored with horseradish.

Octopus goes down really well with my customers. It's definitely one of those things they eat when they are out, because they think it's hard to get right at home. Nonsense, octopus is really simple to do! Follow my recipe, and you will wonder why you haven't tried it before. The lovely Spanish romesco sauce works really well with the caramelized octopus.

Braised octopus with romesco sauce

Serves 4

1 octopus (double sucker
  species), about 2¼ lb [1 kg]
  (defrosted if frozen)
Olive oil for cooking
1 onion, peeled and chopped
4 garlic cloves, peeled and
  chopped
3 bay leaves
1 Tbsp sweet smoked paprika
Sea salt and freshly ground
  black pepper

For the romesco sauce
1 slice crustless white bread
3 Tbsp olive oil
3 red bell peppers, quartered,
  cored, and seeded
7oz [200 g] ripe plum
  tomatoes, halved
¼ cup [30 g] blanched
  almonds
¼ cup [30 g] skinned
  hazelnuts
2 garlic cloves, peeled and
  chopped
2 Tbsp sherry vinegar
14 oz [400 g] canned
  cannellini beans
1 bunch of scallions, sliced

To serve
Sweet smoked paprika
  to sprinkle

Heat a pan large enough to hold the octopus, and add a generous drizzle of olive oil. When hot, add the onion, garlic, bay leaves, and smoked paprika and cook for 2 minutes. Add the whole octopus, and some salt and pepper. Put the lid on, and cook for 1 hour, or until the octopus is tender. To check, insert a knife into a tentacle; it should cut through with ease. If not, continue to cook, checking every 10 minutes until it is ready.

Meanwhile, make the sauce. Preheat your broiler to high. Blitz the bread in a blender to crumbs. Oil and season the peppers and tomatoes all over, then lay skin-side up on a large broiler pan. Broil until the skins are blistered and blackened. Peel away the skins when cool enough to handle.

Place a skillet over medium heat, and add a drizzle of olive oil. When it is hot, add the nuts and fry, stirring occasionally, until golden all over. Tip out onto a plate, and leave to cool. Heat a little more oil in the pan and fry the bread crumbs and garlic until golden and crisp.

Put the garlicky crumbs into a blender, add the tomatoes, peppers, and nuts, and pulse to a rough paste. Add the sherry vinegar with some salt and pepper, and blend for 10 seconds. Transfer to a bowl, and set aside.

When the octopus is cooked, lift it out onto a tray, and leave until cool enough to handle. Reserve the stock. Cut off and reserve the tentacles. Slit open the main body and remove the ink sac, stomach, and eyes carefully. Chop all the main body meat up and set aside.

When ready to serve, in a large pan, mix the cooled, chopped octopus body meat into the sauce. Add the beans, scallions and a cup [240 ml] of the octopus stock (or more if you prefer a "soupy" dish). Heat through.

Meanwhile, place a skillet over high heat. Oil and season the tentacles. When the pan is hot, add a little oil, then the tentacles. Cook for 2 minutes on each side until nicely colored and lightly charred.

Season the stew and share between 4 bowls. Slice the tentacles and share between the bowls. Sprinkle generously with smoked paprika and serve.

SEAFOOD
SALADS

I love the texture of octopus, when it is cooked perfectly. In this salad, the char from broiling it, combined with the smooth softness of the avocado, adds to the excitement. The double sucker species of octopus is the best one to use, as it cooks really well. Most of the time, octopus comes frozen, but that's not a bad thing. In fact, the freezing process helps to tenderize the meat. You could also make this salad with squid.

Octopus, avocado, and tomato salad, lime and cilantro dressing

Serves 4 as an appetizer or light lunch

1 octopus (double sucker species), about 2¼ lb [1 kg] (defrosted if frozen)
Olive oil for cooking
1 white onion, peeled and roughly chopped
4 garlic cloves, peeled and crushed
2 rosemary sprigs
Finely grated zest and juice of 1 lime
Scant ½ cup [100 ml] white wine
Sea salt and freshly ground black pepper

For the salad

2 ripe avocados
20 cherry or baby plum tomatoes, halved
4 packed cups [100 g] arugula leaves

For the lime and cilantro dressing

⅔ cup [150 ml] extra virgin olive oil
Zest and juice of 1 lime
1 Tbsp Dijon mustard
2 Tbsp chopped cilantro

Heat a pan large enough to hold the octopus and add a drizzle of olive oil. When hot, add the onion, garlic, rosemary, and lime zest. Sweat for 3 minutes, then add the octopus, wine, and lime juice. Put the lid on the pan, and simmer gently for 1 hour, or until the octopus is tender. To check, insert a knife into one of the tentacles; it should cut through with ease. If not, continue to cook, checking every 10 minutes, until it is ready.

When the octopus is cooked, lift it out onto a tray, and leave until cool enough to handle. Cut off and reserve the tentacles. Slit open the main body, and remove the ink sac, stomach, and eyes carefully. Cut the meat into strips, thread onto a skewer, and set aside.

Heat up a grill pan or barbecue. Meanwhile, halve, pit, and peel the avocados, then cut into slices, and place in a bowl with the tomatoes, and mix gently.

Oil the octopus pieces and tentacles, and season with salt and pepper. Place both the skewered meat and tentacles on the grill pan or barbecue, and cook for 5 to 6 minutes, until the outside is caramelized and golden.

Meanwhile, to make the dressing, whisk the ingredients together in a bowl, and season with salt and pepper to taste.

Remove the octopus from the skewers, and add to the tomato and avocado with the tentacles. Add a few spoonfuls of dressing, and toss gently, then add the arugula leaves and a pinch of salt. Share the salad equally between 4 plates, and finish with another drizzle of dressing.

Squid is a crowd pleaser for sure! Crumbed, or battered and deep-fried, it always flies off any menu, but to me, it has so much more to offer. For this salad I have quickly poached small squid, and lightly pickled them, before tossing with shaved cauliflower, spicy salami, and peppery watercress. It can be served cold, warm, or hot—the choice is yours.

Squid, watercress, and cauliflower salad with salami

Serves 4 as an appetizer or light lunch

21 oz [600 g] small squid, cleaned, body cut into rings, fins scored

2 garlic cloves, peeled and chopped

1 small cauliflower, finely sliced (ideally on a mandoline)

A bunch of watercress, leaves picked

About 5½ oz [150 g] spicy salami, sliced, and cut into strips

For the dressing

⅔ cup [150 ml] extra virgin olive oil

⅓ cup [75 ml] white wine vinegar

1 red onion, peeled and finely sliced

Sea salt and freshly ground black pepper

For the dressing, whisk the olive oil and wine vinegar together in a large bowl, then add the red onion, and some salt and pepper. Set aside.

In a saucepan, bring around 4½ cups [1 L] of water to a boil, and season generously with salt. Add the garlic, and simmer for 2 minutes. Add the squid to the water, and blanch for 30 seconds, then remove and drain well. Drop the squid straight into the dressing and mix together. Leave to cool.

When ready to serve, add the cauliflower and watercress to the squid mixture along with the salami. Toss to combine, and season with salt and pepper to taste. Serve immediately.

This is a perfect, simple salad for a summer's day, especially when tomatoes are plentiful, juicy, and sweet. It's always nice to cook your own crab, but if you can get hold of a good one, freshly picked, you can assemble the salad in next to no time. The horseradish adds a refreshing hot kick, and really brings the salad alive.

Crab and tomato salad with horseradish dressing

Serves 4 as an appetizer

About 10½ oz [300 g] white crabmeat (from a 3¼ lb [1.5 kg] freshly cooked crab)
12 ripe tomatoes (the best variety you can get)
1 shallot, peeled and minced
Scant ½ cup [100 ml] olive oil
3½ Tbsp white wine vinegar
1 tsp superfine sugar
1 Tbsp chopped parsley
Sea salt and freshly ground black pepper

For the horseradish dressing

⅔ cup [150 ml] sour cream
2 Tbsp creamed horseradish
Finely grated zest and juice of 1 lemon
3½ oz [100 g] brown crabmeat, strained

To garnish

Zest of 1 lemon (microplaned)
2 Tbsp flat-leaf parsley leaves, sliced

Bring a pan of water (large enough to hold all the tomatoes) to a boil. Remove the cores from the tomatoes, and score a cross in the skin on the top of each one. Lower the tomatoes into the boiling water, and blanch for 20 seconds, then remove to a tray. When cool enough to handle, peel off the skins. Cut half of the tomatoes into ⅛ in [3 mm] slices; cut the rest into wedges.

Place all the tomatoes in a bowl and add the shallot, olive oil, wine vinegar, sugar, and chopped parsley. Toss gently to mix, and season with salt and pepper to taste. Set aside.

Check through the white crabmeat carefully for fragments of shell or cartilage. Place the crabmeat in a bowl, and season with salt and pepper.

For the dressing, whisk the ingredients together in a bowl until smoothly combined. Season with salt and pepper to taste.

To serve, divide the tomato salad between 4 plates. Share the white crabmeat equally between the plates, and drizzle the dressing over the salad. Finish with a sprinkling of lemon zest and parsley.

Seafood salads

Potatoes, chiles and shrimp sit so well together in this effortless, comforting salad. I like to eat it just as it is, but you could serve it as a side salad if you like. I have also made it with crab, lobster, and scallops—all work brilliantly. I make it quite spicy, so if you don't like the heat, you might want to cut down on the chiles. It is really versatile, and can be served hot, warm, or cold. I love it!

Shrimp, chile, and potato salad

Serves 4 as an appetizer or light lunch

21 oz [600 g] large raw shrimp, peeled and deveined
14 oz [400 g] small new potatoes
Sunflower oil for cooking
4 scallions, trimmed and sliced
2 Tbsp finely sliced cilantro, plus extra leaves to serve
1 Tbsp finely sliced mint, plus extra leaves to serve
Sea salt and freshly ground black pepper

For the sauce

Sunflower oil for cooking
1 red onion, peeled and minced
3 garlic cloves, peeled, halved (germ removed) and chopped
2 red chiles, seeded and chopped
1 tsp black onion seeds
1 tsp coriander seeds
4 ripe tomatoes, core removed, seeded, and chopped
Sea salt and freshly ground black pepper

First make the sauce. Heat a skillet over medium heat and add a drizzle of sunflower oil. When it is hot, add the onion, garlic, chiles, and spices and fry for 3 to 4 minutes until the mixture begins to color. Add the chopped tomatoes, season with salt and pepper, and cook for 6 to 8 minutes until they begin to collapse.

Transfer the contents of the pan to a food processor, and blend until the mixture is as smooth as you can get it. Pass through a strainer into a clean bowl, and allow to cool.

Add the shrimp to the cooled sauce, and leave to marinate for at least 10 minutes, longer if you have the time.

To cook the new potatoes, put them into a pan, cover with water, and add a pinch of salt. Bring to a boil, then reduce the heat, and simmer for 10 to 15 minutes until they are cooked. Drain thoroughly, and leave to cool slightly while you cook the shrimp.

Heat a skillet over high heat. Remove the shrimp from the sauce with a slotted spoon, keeping the sauce. Add a drizzle of oil to the hot pan, then carefully add the shrimp, and cook for 2 minutes on each side.

Add the sauce to the pan, and bring to a simmer, then take off the heat. Stir in the scallions, cilantro, and mint. Now add the potatoes (or combine in a bowl if your pan is too small). Season the shrimp salad with salt and pepper to taste, and toss well.

Serve the salad scattered with extra cilantro and mint leaves, either on its own, or with a green salad if you prefer.

Seafood salads

Sometimes, perfectly cooked simple seafood and good mayonnaise is all you need to impress. If you are entertaining, this is often the best way to go, as everything can be done in advance. Remember to remove this dish from the fridge half an hour or so before serving, to take the chill off the lobsters. Verjus gives seafood a lovely fresh acidity.

Dressed lobster with herb mayonnaise

Serves 2 as a light lunch

2 live lobsters, up to 2¼ lb
  [1 kg] each
2 shallots, peeled and sliced
1 fennel bulb, trimmed and
  sliced
2 carrots, pared and sliced
2 garlic cloves, peeled and
  crushed
2 thyme sprigs
2 bay leaves
10 black peppercorns
⅞ cup [200 ml] verjus
Olive oil to drizzle
Salt

For the herb mayonnaise

2 egg yolks
1 tsp English mustard
1 small garlic clove, peeled
  and chopped
1 shallot, peeled and minced
1½ Tbsp verjus
⅞ cup [200 ml] light olive oil
1 Tbsp chopped chives
1 Tbsp chopped tarragon
Sea salt

Put the lobsters in the freezer for an hour before cooking to sedate them.

To cook the lobsters, put the vegetables, garlic, herbs, peppercorns, and verjus into a large pan (big enough to hold both the lobsters). Pour in enough water to cover the lobsters, and add plenty of salt. Bring to a boil over high heat, then reduce the heat, and simmer for 5 minutes.

In the meantime, take the lobsters out of the freezer and firmly insert the tip of a strong chef's knife into the cross on the head to kill each one instantly. Add the lobsters to the simmering bouillon, and cook for 6 minutes, then remove the pan from the heat.

Leave the lobsters in the bouillon for 2 minutes to finish cooking in the residual heat, then lift them out. Strain the bouillon, and let it cool. Place the lobsters on a tray, and leave to cool completely.

Meanwhile, make the mayonnaise. Put the egg yolks, mustard, garlic, shallot, and verjus into a bowl, and whisk together for 1 minute. Add the olive oil in a thin, steady steam, whisking as you do so, until it is all incorporated. Season with salt to taste, cover, and place in the fridge.

When the lobsters are cold, carefully cut them in half lengthwise, from head to tail. Remove the stomach sac from the head, and the dark intestinal thread that runs along the length of the tail. Crack the claws and knuckles, and place the lobsters on a large platter.

When ready to serve, mix the chopped herbs into the mayonnaise, and spoon some into the head part of the shell. Drizzle the lobsters with a little bouillon and olive oil. Serve at once, with the rest of the mayonnaise in a bowl on the side.

This lovely, summery dish is really quick to knock up. Red mullet (goatfish) is such a treat, and the eggplant and basil go perfectly—to give the dish a Mediterranean feel. You can also turn this into a really great pasta meal. Just boil some linguine, and pan-fry the fish, then add the salad and dressing. If red mullet is unavailable, substitute bream or bass.

Red mullet and eggplant salad with basil dressing

Serves 4 as an appetizer or light lunch

4 red mullet (goatfish), 10½ to 14 oz [300 to 400 g] each, scaled, gutted, and butterfly filleted
Olive oil for cooking
Sea salt and freshly ground black pepper

For the eggplant salad
⅓ cup [75 ml] olive oil
2 red onions, peeled and sliced
2 eggplants, peeled and diced
⅓ cup [75 ml] balsamic vinegar
2 handfuls of arugula leaves
2 Tbsp pine nuts
¾ cup [100 g] green olives, pitted and sliced
A little extra virgin olive oil to dress

For the basil dressing
1 shallot, peeled and finely sliced
1 garlic clove, peeled, halved (germ removed), and minced
4 anchovy fillets in oil, drained and minced
Heaping ⅓ cup [50 g] green olives, pitted and chopped
A bunch of basil, picked
⅔ cup [150 ml] olive oil
⅓ cup [75 ml] white wine vinegar

First make the dressing. Put the shallot, garlic, anchovies, and olives in a food processor and blitz for 1 minute. Add the basil, and blitz for another minute, then scrape down the sides of the bowl. Now, with the motor running, pour in the olive oil in a thin, steady stream through the funnel. Finally, add the wine vinegar, and season to taste with salt and pepper. Set aside.

For the salad, heat a large pan (with a tight-fitting lid) over medium heat, and add the olive oil. When it is hot, add the red onions, and cook for 5 minutes until they start to soften. Next, add the eggplants, and give the mixture a good stir. Cover and cook for 5 minutes, stirring a couple of times.

Add the balsamic vinegar, and cook, uncovered, for another 3 minutes, or until the eggplant is cooked. Spoon the mixture onto a tray, and allow to cool.

Preheat the broiler to cook the fish. Lay the butterflied red mullet fillets skin-side up on an oiled broiler pan, and season all over with salt and pepper. Place the fillets under the broiler, and cook for 4 minutes.

While the fish is cooking, transfer the eggplant mixture to a bowl, and add the arugula, pine nuts, and olives. Toss to mix, and season the salad with salt and pepper. Dress with a drizzle of good olive oil.

Share the salad between 4 plates. When cooked, lay a butterflied red mullet on top of each portion, and drizzle the basil dressing around the plates. Serve immediately.

I generally use very good quality farmed salmon for this dish, rather than wild salmon, which is something of a delicacy these days. Kohlrabi lends a nice crunchy texture, and earthy freshness to the salad, and makes it more of a wintry dish. If you wanted to serve it as a summer salad, you could replace the kohlrabi with refreshing cucumber, or ripe tomatoes.

Salmon and kohlrabi tartare salad

Serves 6 to 8 as an appetizer or light lunch

1 side of good quality farmed or wild salmon, pin-boned

For the court bouillon

3 shallots, peeled and sliced
2 carrots, pared and sliced
2 bay leaves
A few thyme sprigs
3 Tbsp sea salt
⅔ cup [150 ml] verjus
A handful of parsley
8 cups [2 L] water
1 tsp black peppercorns

For the kohlrabi tartare salad

1 red onion, finely sliced
3 Tbsp verjus
2 kohlrabi, peeled, halved, and finely sliced (ideally on a mandoline)
1 Tbsp capers in brine, rinsed
2 large gherkins, thinly sliced
1 Tbsp each chopped curly parsley, tarragon, chervil, and chives
⅓ cup [75 ml] cold-pressed canola oil
Sea salt and freshly ground black pepper

For the salad cream

2 egg yolks
2 tsp English mustard
2 tsp superfine sugar
2 Tbsp verjus
Scant ½ cup [100 ml] cold-pressed canola oil
1 Tbsp each chopped curly parsley, tarragon, chervil, and chives
⅔ cup [150 ml] heavy cream

To make the court bouillon for poaching the salmon, put the shallots, carrots, bay leaves, thyme, salt, verjus, and parsley into a pan, and cover with the water. Bring to a boil, skim off any impurities, and simmer for 15 minutes. Add the peppercorns, and remove from the heat.

For the salad, put the red onion into a large bowl, add the verjus, and set aside for 10 minutes or so to mingle and soften.

Preheat your oven to 400°F [200°C].

To make the salad cream, put the egg yolks, mustard, sugar, and verjus into a bowl, and whisk for 1 minute, then gradually whisk in the oil, drop by drop to begin with, until you have an emulsion, then add the rest in a thin stream. To finish, whisk in the herbs and cream, and season with salt and pepper to taste. Cover, and refrigerate until ready to serve.

Bring the court bouillon back to a simmer. Meanwhile, for the salad, add the sliced kohlrabi to the red onion, followed by the capers, gherkins, and herbs. Toss well, and season with salt and pepper to taste.

Cut the salmon in half to fit into a deep roasting pan. Line the pan with baking parchment or silicone paper, and lay the salmon on top. Pour the contents of the court bouillon pan over the salmon, and place in the oven. Cook for 12 to 14 minutes, then carefully remove the pan from the oven, and lift the salmon onto a plate to cool. When cool enough to handle, flake the salmon into nice chunks.

To serve, spoon three-quarters of the kohlrabi onto a large platter, then add the chunks of poached salmon. Add the remaining salad, spoon on the salad cream, and serve.

I love the freshness and textures of this salad: the tender zucchini, crunchy nuts, zingy dressing, and oily goodness of the fish. The sardines need to be spanking fresh, but if you can't get hold of any really fresh sardines, then mackerel, sprats, or herring will work. Failing that, I have made this recipe with really good quality canned sardines.

Sardines with zucchini and nut salad

Serves 4 as an appetizer or light lunch

8 sardines, scaled, gutted, and butterfly filleted
Olive oil for cooking
Finely grated zest of 1 lemon
Sea salt and freshly ground black pepper

For the zucchini and nut salad

1 red onion, peeled and finely sliced
3 large zucchini
½ cup [50 g] chopped roasted peanuts
½ cup [50 g] chopped roasted cashews
Heaping ⅓ cup [50 g] pine nuts, toasted
2 Tbsp chopped dill

For the lemon dressing

Scant ½ cup [100 ml] olive oil
Finely grated zest and juice of 1 lemon
Scant ½ cup [100 ml] peanut oil

Preheat your broiler to its highest setting.

For the dressing, whisk the olive oil, lemon zest and juice, and the oil together in a bowl, and season with salt and pepper to taste.

Add the red onion to the dressing, and leave to stand for 10 minutes; this will take the raw edge off the taste.

Meanwhile, using a mandoline if you have one, cut the zucchini into matchsticks, and place in a bowl. Remove the red onion from the dressing with a slotted spoon, and add to the zucchini with 6 Tbsp of the dressing; mix well. Set aside. Reserve the rest of the dressing.

To cook the sardines, lay the butterflied fillets skin side down on an oiled broiler pan. Season the flesh side with salt and pepper, and sprinkle with the lemon zest, then turn the fillets over. Place the pan under the broiler, and cook the fillets skin-side up for about 4 minutes until they are cooked through, then remove from the pan.

Add the cooking juices from the broiler pan to the zucchini, and toss to combine. Add the nuts and chopped dill, mix gently, then share the salad equally between 4 warmed plates. Lay the butterflied sardines on top, and drizzle with the rest of the dressing.

Seafood salads

I adore mackerel, and my favorite food to eat out is Asian, so I was keen to bring the two together. I created this salad for a party at home from the Asian ingredients I had in my kitchen cupboards. The texture of the mackerel and its natural oiliness work beautifully with the Asian flavorings. Saying that, you could put any oily fish with this dish—sardines would be a fantastic alternative.

Mackerel and noodle salad, cashew and lime dressing

Serves 4

4 mackerel, filleted, trimmed, and pin-boned
4½ cups [1 L] sunflower oil, for deep-frying
3 banana shallots, finely sliced, separated into rings
¾ cup [100 g] all-purpose flour
Heaping ¾ cup [100 g] cashews
Sea salt

For the noodle salad

3¾ cups [300 g] dried noodles
2 large carrots, cut into fine julienne
4 scallions, finely sliced
Scant ½ cup [50 g] grated fresh ginger
4 garlic cloves, peeled and grated
A bunch of radishes, finely sliced
A handful of mint leaves, roughly chopped
A handful of cilantro leaves

For the cashew and lime dressing

Scant ½ cup [100 ml] fish sauce
Zest and juice of 2 limes
6 Tbsp [75 g] palm sugar or soft brown sugar
1 shallot, minced
2 garlic cloves, peeled and grated
1 red chile, halved, seeded, and sliced

Heat the oil for deep-frying in a deep, heavy pan to 350°F [180°C]. Toss the shallot rings through the flour seasoned with salt, shaking off any excess (save for the mackerel). Fry the shallot rings in the hot oil until golden and crisp. Remove with a slotted spoon, and drain on paper towels. Season the shallots with salt, and set aside to cool.

Next, fry the cashews in the oil for 2 to 3 minutes until golden. Lift out with a slotted spoon, and drain on paper towels. Season with salt and set aside.

Pass the mackerel through the flour and knock off any excess. Fry 4 fillets at a time for 3 minutes. Remove and drain on paper towels. Season with salt, and leave to cool.

For the salad, bring a pan of water to a boil, add salt, then drop in the noodles and take off the heat. Leave to soften for 3 minutes, then drain the noodles well in a colander (excess water will dilute the dressing).

Heat a large skillet or wok, and add a drizzle of the oil from the fish pan. When hot, add the carrots, scallions, ginger, and garlic. Stir-fry for 2 minutes, until the veg start to soften. Remove and set aside.

To make the dressing, put the fish sauce, lime juice, and sugar into a pan over medium heat, until the sugar is dissolved. Take off the heat and add the shallot, garlic, chile, and lime zest.

To assemble, put the noodles, stir-fried veg, and dressing into a large bowl, and toss well. Add the radishes, mint, and most of the cilantro and toss again. Taste for seasoning, and add a little more salt if required. Arrange on a large platter or divide between 4 bowls.

Break the mackerel into chunks and place on top of the salad. Finally, scatter over the fried cashews, shallots, and remaining cilantro leaves. Serve at room temperature or warm.

Seafood salads

If you see John Dory at the fish market, buy it. It's a great fish with a delicate texture and delicious sweet flavor, but it's not always available. I like to serve this salad as a springtime lunch dish. The zesty flavors will brighten up your day.

John Dory, shaved asparagus, chile, and orange salad

Serves 4

4 John Dory, about 18 oz
  [500 g] each, gutted, filleted,
  and skinned
2 red onions, peeled
16 asparagus spears, woody
  parts removed
4 red chiles, halved, seeded,
  and thinly sliced
1 orange
Sea salt and freshly ground
  black pepper

For the dressing
4 Tbsp verjus
4 Tbsp olive oil
1 Tbsp Dijon mustard
1 Tbsp honey
2 Tbsp cilantro leaves,
  chopped
2 Tbsp mint leaves, chopped

Preheat the broiler to high, ready to cook the fish.

Using a mandoline if you have one, slice the red onions and asparagus as thinly as possible and place in a large bowl with the sliced chiles. Finely grate the zest of the orange and add to the salad. Cut away the peel and pith from the orange, and cut out the sections from between the membranes; add to the salad, and toss to combine.

For the dressing, whisk the ingredients together in a bowl, and season with salt and pepper.

Add half of the dressing to the asparagus salad, and toss lightly. Taste and add more seasoning if required.

Season the fish all over with salt and pepper, then lay on the broiler pan. Place under the broiler for 3 minutes, then turn the fillets over, and cook the other side for 3 minutes.

To serve, share most of the asparagus salad between 4 warmed plates. Place a broiled fish fillet on top, arrange the remaining salad on the fish, and drizzle over the reserved dressing. Serve immediately.

Seafood salads

As soon as parsnips are at their best, you've just got to try this warm, autumnal salad. The cod and bacon flavors work really well with parsnip and kale. I like to flake the broiled cod through the salad, but you could leave it as a whole fillet if you prefer. The salad is also delicious with carrots in place of the parsnips.

Cod, bacon, kale, and parsnip salad

Serves 4

21 oz [600 g] cod fillet, skinned and pin-boned
2 large parsnips
Olive oil for cooking and to dress
1 garlic clove, peeled and roughly chopped
⅓ cup [75 g] butter
7 oz [200 g] kale, stalks removed
6 slices of smoked bacon
4 tsp chopped parsley
Finely grated zest and juice of 1 lemon
Sea salt and freshly ground black pepper

Peel the parsnips, and slice each one lengthwise into 8 ribbons. Place a large skillet over medium heat, and add a drizzle of olive oil. When hot, add the garlic and parsnips, and cook for 2 to 3 minutes, until the parsnips start to color. Now add the butter, and some salt and pepper. Cook for another 5 to 6 minutes, until the parsnips are golden and starting to soften. Remove the parsnips and garlic to a tray lined with paper towels to drain; keep warm.

Preheat your broiler to its highest setting, ready to cook the fish.

Wipe out the skillet, put it back over a medium-high heat, and add another drizzle of olive oil. When the oil is hot, add the kale, and stir-fry for 3 to 4 minutes until it is cooked, but still retains some bite. Transfer to the same tray as the parsnips; keep warm.

Place the bacon slices and cod fillets on a well-oiled broiler pan. Season the fish with salt and pepper, and put the pan under the broiler. Cook the cod fillets for 3 minutes, then turn them over, and cook for an additional 2 minutes. Remove the fish as soon as it is cooked, and the bacon when it is well colored and cooked.

Chop the bacon and place it in a large bowl. Chop the kale and add it to the bowl. Next flake the cod and add it too. Finally, add the parsnips, garlic, parsley, lemon zest and juice, and a drizzle of olive oil. Season the salad with salt and pepper to taste, then carefully toss it all together.

Share the salad between 4 warmed plates and serve immediately.

Seafood salads

Smoked fish and pickles work so well together. The acidity of the pickle cuts the richness of the fish with every mouthful, to delicious effect. If you prepare the pickled veg in advance, you can assemble this salad in 5 minutes—perfect for a quick lunch. If you're feeling like showing off though, you can top the salad with some freshly broiled mackerel fillets.

Smoked mackerel and pickled vegetable salad

Serves 4

6 smoked mackerel fillets
2 tsp creamed horseradish
Finely grated zest and juice
  of 1 lime

**For the pickled vegetable
  salad**
Scant ½ cup [100 ml] hard
  cider
Scant ½ cup [100 ml] cider
  vinegar
Scant ½ cup [100 ml] water
½ cup [100 g] superfine sugar
1 banana shallot, peeled and
  sliced into rings
1 carrot, pared and thinly
  sliced
1 fennel bulb, tough outer
  layer removed, shredded
  (ideally on a mandoline)
1 celery stalk, strings removed
  (with a peeler) and finely
  sliced
1 red bell pepper, skinned,
  cored, seeded, and finely
  sliced
1 garlic clove, peeled and
  crushed
Sea salt and freshly ground
  black pepper

To serve
Cold-pressed canola oil
  to drizzle
Peppergrass cress or salad
  leaves

For the pickled vegetables, put the hard cider, cider vinegar, water, and sugar into a pan over medium heat to dissolve the sugar. Put all the prepared vegetables and garlic into a bowl large enough to hold them and the pickling liquor. Bring the pickling liquor to a boil, then pour over the vegetables. Cover the bowl with plastic wrap, and set aside to cool.

To prepare the fish, remove the skin and cut down the middle of the fillet to cut out all the little bones. Flake the fish into a bowl and mix in the horseradish, lime zest, and juice.

Drain the pickled vegetables, keeping the liquor to store any leftovers.

Gently toss the pickled vegetables with the mackerel, adding a drizzle of canola oil. Taste for seasoning, adding salt and/or pepper if need be.

To serve, share the salad equally between 4 plates, and finish with a drizzle of canola oil, and cress or salad leaves.

BAKE

Cooking for a crowd is always a bit daunting, even for me! This shrimp dish looks, smells, and tastes amazing, and is really simple to cook for a lot of people, providing you have the space. Try and find good quality sustainable shrimp—it will make all the difference, trust me.

Salt and seaweed baked shrimp, tomato and cilantro salad

Serves 6

30 large raw shrimp, peeled and deveined, but heads and tails left on
Olive oil to drizzle
2 good handfuls of dried seaweed
About 18 oz [500 g] rock salt for baking

For the tomato and cilantro salad
20 ripe plum tomatoes, halved
1 bunch of scallions, trimmed and sliced
⅓ cup [75 ml] white wine vinegar
Scant ½ cup [100 ml] olive oil
1 tsp ground coriander
½ tsp cayenne pepper
A handful of cilantro, leaves picked and chopped
Sea salt and freshly ground black pepper

Preheat your oven to 400°F [200°C].

For the salad, put the tomatoes, scallions, wine vinegar, and olive oil into a bowl. Season with the ground coriander cayenne, and some salt and black pepper. Toss to mix and set aside.

Toss the shrimp in a bowl with a little salt and a drizzle of olive oil.

Scatter the seaweed and rock salt in a large roasting pan. Lay the shrimp on top and bake for 5 minutes, depending on the size of your shrimp.

Meanwhile, add the cilantro to the salad and toss together.

Remove the pan of shrimp from the oven, and place on a mat on the table. Eat immediately, using your hands. No time for cutlery, but provide bowls and forks for the salad, and finger bowls.

I'm particularly fond of baked scallops. Like many of my recipes, I came up with this one at home, after rummaging through the cupboards to see what I could find. Cooking the scallops in this way protects the delicate meat from direct heat, giving you a lovely soft cooked texture. Feel free to vary the flavorings for the crumbs and butter as you like.

Scallops with Cheddar crumbs, smoked paprika and cilantro butter

Serves 4 as an appetizer

12 fresh scallops, shelled and cleaned (shells reserved)
1 cup [240 ml] white wine

For the crumbs

6 to 8 slices [200 g] crustless good quality bread
A handful of cilantro, leaves picked
Scant 1 cup [75 g] grated sharp Cheddar cheese

For the smoked paprika and cilantro butter

10½ oz [300 g] unsalted butter, cut into cubes and softened
1 banana shallot or 2 standard shallots, peeled and minced
1 garlic clove, peeled, halved (germ removed), and minced
2 tsp sweet smoked paprika
A handful of cilantro, leaves picked and minced
Sea salt

To serve

1 lime, cut into wedges

Preheat your oven to 425°F [220°C]. Clean the best 12 scallop shells, dry well, and reserve for cooking.

To make the crumbs, blitz the bread and cilantro in a food processor until the bread is reduced to crumbs, and the cilantro is minced. Add the cheese, and blitz for 30 seconds. Transfer to a tray, and set aside.

For the butter, put the soft butter into a bowl with the shallot(s), garlic, smoked paprika, and chopped cilantro. Mix well to combine, and season with salt to taste. Set aside until ready to cook.

When ready to eat, place one scallop in each of the reserved shells. Sprinkle 4 tsp white wine and dot 2 Tbsp butter on each one. Scatter the crumbs evenly over the top and place the scallops on a large oven pan. (You may need to use 2 pans.)

Bake the scallops for 6 to 8 minutes. To check that they are cooked, insert a small knife into the center of a scallop, and hold it there for 10 seconds. Pull the knife out, and place it on the back of your hand; if the blade feels hot, they are ready. (It should not be piping hot.)

Serve the scallops immediately, with lime wedges.

This is a version of the Oysters Rockefeller that we cook at Outlaw's Fish Kitchen. The Porthilly oysters we use are fantastic for cooking, and great in this dish. If you have any of the flavored butter left over, wrap it well and freeze it, but I doubt you will—it tastes too good.

Baked oysters with watercress and anise butter

Serves 4

24 live rock oysters
About 18 oz [500 g] rock
 salt for baking
Scant 1¾ cups [100 g] fresh
 bread crumbs

**For the watercress and
 anise butter**
1½ bunches [150 g]
 watercress, leaves picked
3 large handfuls [150 g]
 spinach leaves
⅔ cup [150 g] unsalted butter
3 small shallots, minced
1 small green chile, seeded
 and minced
2 Tbsp Ricard Pernod anise-
 flavored liqueur
1½ cups [30 g] tarragon
 leaves

To serve
Rock salt or seaweed

For the butter, bring a pan of salted water to a boil. Add the watercress and spinach, and blanch for 1 minute. Immediately drain and plunge the leaves into a bowl of ice water to cool quickly. When cold, drain and squeeze out the excess water.

Heat a small pan over medium heat, and add one-third of the butter. When it is bubbling, add the shallots and chile, and sweat for 3 minutes until the shallots are translucent. Add the Pernod, and simmer for 30 seconds.

Transfer the contents of the pan to a blender. Let cool slightly, then add the tarragon and blanched watercress and spinach. Blitz to combine, then add the remaining butter. Blend for 30 seconds, scraping down the sides of the blender container once or twice. Transfer to a bowl, cover, and set aside.

Preheat your oven to 400°F [200°C]. Line a large baking pan with enough salt to allow you to sit the oyster shells on without them toppling over. Open the oysters, and prise off the top shell. Drain off the juices. Cut the muscle to release the oyster, but leave it in the rounded shell; check for any fragments of shell.

Top each oyster with a generous helping of the watercress butter, and sprinkle with an even layer of bread crumbs. Bake for 12 minutes, or until the bread crumbs are golden and crispy. Serve immediately, on little salt mounds, or nestled in seaweed.

This is a great way to cook those medium or slightly larger squid, which are perfect for a single portion filled with a tasty stuffing. The stuffing in this recipe isn't supposed to all stay inside the squid pouches; some of it will ooze out to create a delicious sauce. I'd suggest serving this dish with a simple arugula salad, dressed with a little balsamic vinegar and olive oil.

Stuffed squid, red peppers, chickpeas, olives, and sherry

Serves 4

4 medium squid, bodies 8 to 10 in [20 to 25 cm] long, cleaned, and tentacles reserved
Olive oil for cooking and to drizzle
2 shallots, peeled and minced
3 garlic cloves, peeled and minced
2 red bell peppers, peeled, cored, seeded, and diced
4 ripe plum tomatoes, cored, and each cut into 6 pieces
1 cup [100 g] pitted black olives, quartered
14 oz [400 g] canned chickpeas, drained and rinsed
16 basil leaves, finely sliced
2⅛ cups [500 ml] dry sherry
Scant ½ cup [100 g] unsalted butter, diced
2⅛ cups [500 ml] fish stock (see page 218)
Sea salt and freshly ground black pepper

Preheat your oven to 400°F [200°C].

Place a sauté pan over medium heat, and add a generous drizzle of olive oil. When hot, add the shallots, garlic, and red peppers, and sweat for 5 minutes. Add the tomatoes and olives, and cook for an additional 5 minutes, until the tomatoes soften and begin to collapse. Season with salt and pepper to taste.

Add the chickpeas, and cook for an additional 10 minutes. Remove from the heat, and allow to cool.

Lay the cleaned squid pouches in an oven pan, and season all over with salt and pepper. Season the tentacles too, but set these aside on a plate.

When the stuffing mixture is cool, stir through most of the sliced basil. Now, using a spoon, fill each squid pouch with as much stuffing as it will take. If there is any stuffing mixture left, add that to the pan too.

Pour the sherry over the stuffed squid, and dot with the butter. Bake for 15 to 20 minutes, basting with the mixture every 5 minutes. Pour on the fish stock, and cook for another 10 minutes, adding the tentacles to the pan for the final 5 minutes.

Place a stuffed squid pouch on each warmed plate with the tentacles alongside, and spoon on some of the sauce. Scatter over the remaining sliced basil, add a drizzle of olive oil, and serve immediately.

For me, baking and steaming are the best ways to cook haddock. That's why fish and chips are so good—the fish steams inside its protective batter jacket. Other cooking techniques seem to dry out the fish too much. I'm a fan of béarnaise sauce, so I decided to create a simple butter with the same flavors. It marries so well with the fish, tomatoes, and mushrooms, bringing the whole dish together. You can use cod, hake, or really fresh whiting in place of the haddock, if you like.

Haddock baked in a bag with béarnaise butter

Serves 4

4 filleted haddock portions, about 5½ oz [150 g] each
8 small portobello mushrooms, peeled, and stem removed
4 plum tomatoes, halved
Olive oil for cooking
4 garlic cloves, peeled, halved (germ removed), and minced
Sea salt and freshly ground black pepper

For the béarnaise butter

9 oz [250 g] unsalted butter, diced and softened
2 shallots, peeled and minced
A handful of tarragon, leaves picked and minced
1 tsp cracked black or coarsely ground black pepper
1 tsp sea salt
2 Tbsp red wine vinegar

Preheat your oven to 425°F [220°C].

To make the béarnaise butter, put the butter, shallots, tarragon, black pepper, salt, and wine vinegar into a bowl and mix until evenly combined. Taste and adjust the seasoning if necessary. Cover, and set aside.

To cook the mushrooms and tomatoes, line a baking pan with two layers of aluminum foil, making sure they overlap the edges of the pan. Drizzle the top sheet of foil with olive oil, and sprinkle with salt and pepper. Place the mushrooms and tomatoes on the foil and season them too. Sprinkle with the chopped garlic. Place the pan in the oven, and cook for 10 minutes.

To cook the fish, take the pan from the oven, and give the tomatoes and mushrooms a squeeze to check that they are nearly cooked. Season the haddock with salt and pepper, and drizzle generously with olive oil. Place the haddock skin-side up on top of the mushrooms and tomatoes. Spread some of the béarnaise butter on top of the haddock.

Cover the fish with two more sheets of foil and fold the top and bottom foil edges together to make a sealed package. Place the pan back in the oven, and cook for 12 minutes. Remove the pan from the oven and rest for 2 minutes.

To serve, carefully cut open the foil at the top (don't let the steam scald you). Using a fish spatula, carefully lift the fish onto 4 warmed plates. Share the tomatoes and mushrooms equally between the plates, and spoon the buttery sauce over the fish. Serve immediately.

Turbot is such a great fish to bake. Here I'm coating it with a seaweed and bread crumb crust, which adds flavor, and protects the fish from the direct heat of the oven. It's also perfect for soaking up the turbot's natural cooking juices. Using olive oil instead of butter in the classic hollandaise works really well—do give it a try. I like to serve this dish simply with boiled new potatoes and broccoli.

Turbot fillets, seaweed crust, olive oil and lime hollandaise

Serves 4

4 filleted turbot portions, about 6½ oz [180 g] each, skinned
¾ cup [100 g] all-purpose flour, to dust
2 large eggs, beaten
Sea salt and freshly ground black pepper

For the seaweed crust
Scant 1¾ cups [100 g] fresh bread crumbs
2 Tbsp dried seaweed flakes
2 Tbsp chopped flat-leaf parsley
Finely grated zest of 1 lime

For the lime hollandaise
¾ cup [175 ml] olive oil
Finely grated zest and juice of 1 lime
2 egg yolks
2 Tbsp water

Preheat your oven to 425°F [220°C].

For the seaweed crust, put the bread crumbs, seaweed, parsley, and lime zest into a food processor with a pinch of salt and a generous grinding of black pepper. Blitz until the bread crumbs start to go green, but don't overwork. Tip the bread crumb mixture out onto a tray.

Check your fish fillets for any bone or sinew. Have the flour ready on a plate, and the beaten eggs in a shallow bowl. One by one, dip one side of each fillet into the flour, then dip the same side into the egg. Finally lay the turbot fillets, coated side down, in the seaweed crumb mix, and pat down gently. Leave the fillets like this until you are ready to cook them.

To make the lime hollandaise, warm the olive oil in a pan until lukewarm, then add half the lime zest, and remove from the heat. Place the egg yolks in a medium heatproof bowl, and add the lime juice and water. Stand the bowl over a pan of gently simmering water and whisk until the mixture thickens enough to form a ribbon when the beaters are lifted.

Remove the bowl from the pan, and slowly whisk in the olive oil, in a thin, steady stream. Once all the oil is incorporated, season the hollandaise with salt and pepper to taste. Cover with plastic wrap to prevent a skin forming, and keep warm while you cook the fish.

To cook the fish, place the turbot fillets, crust uppermost, on an oiled baking pan and bake for 8 to 10 minutes until the fish is just cooked.

Carefully lift each turbot fillet onto a warmed plate. Sprinkle with the remaining lime zest, and serve immediately, with the lime hollandaise.

These flatbreads go down well whenever I cook them for friends—I think it's because everyone loves a pizza, and they come pretty close. Sardines work well, because of the lovely oiliness you get from them, but herrings or mackerel would be good too. You can vary the topping ingredients, but make sure the mixture isn't too wet, or the bread will be soggy. For a party, you could make a large flatbread—it will look amazing.

Sardine, pepper, and shallot flatbreads

Makes 4

8 sardines, scaled, gutted, and filleted
A little light olive oil, for oiling and drizzling
Sea salt and freshly ground black pepper

For the flatbread dough
Heaping 1¾ cups [250 g] self-rising flour, plus extra to dust
2 tsp sea salt
1⅛ cups [250 g] full-fat Greek yogurt
1 Tbsp chopped tender rosemary leaves
2 Tbsp grated sharp Cheddar cheese
1 garlic clove, peeled and chopped

For the topping
3½ Tbsp olive oil
3½ Tbsp unsalted butter
4 banana shallots, peeled and sliced
2 red bell peppers, peeled, seeded, and sliced
2 garlic cloves, peeled and sliced
1 tender rosemary sprig, leaves picked and chopped
⅓ cup [75 ml] red wine vinegar
¼ cup [50 g] superfine sugar
1 Tbsp small capers in brine, drained and rinsed
A bunch of basil, leaves picked and shredded

To make the flatbread dough, place all the ingredients in a bowl and mix well until evenly combined, and the mixture forms a dough. Turn out onto a lightly floured surface, and knead for 2 minutes. Cover with a clean damp cloth, and set aside while you make the topping.

For the topping, heat a medium pan over medium heat, and add the olive oil and butter. When hot, add the shallots, peppers, garlic, and rosemary. Cook, stirring, frequently, for 5 minutes, until the veg start to soften. Reduce the heat, and cook gently for an additional 5 minutes.

Now add the wine vinegar and sugar, and cook until the vinegar has reduced right down, then add the capers, and season with salt and pepper to taste. Transfer the mixture to a tray, and set aside to cool.

Preheat your oven to 425°F [220°C], and oil two large baking sheets with olive oil.

Divide the bread dough into 4 equal portions, and shape each into a ball. Roll out each one to a round or oval, ⅛ in [3 mm] thick. Lift onto the oiled sheets.

Stir the shredded basil through the cooled shallot mixture, then divide it between the dough bases, making sure you spread it right to the edges. Bake for 10 minutes.

While the flatbreads are in the oven, oil and season your sardine fillets. Take the flatbreads from the oven, and lay 4 sardine fillets on top of each one. Return to the oven, and bake for an additional 8 minutes.

As you take the flatbreads from the oven, drizzle with a little olive oil. Serve immediately.

Everyone has their own recipe for a fabulous fish pie. For me, it has to be one-third cod, one-third salmon, and one-third smoked haddock. Too much cod and it's bland, too much smoked haddock and it dominates, too much salmon and it's greasy. As for those who make it posh with lobster, shrimp, and scallops, that's just a waste. I've cooked this recipe for two and I've cooked it for 200... I think it's bloody lovely! If you want some veg with it, you can't go wrong with buttered, minted peas and carrots.

My fish pie

Serves 8

For the mashed potato
3¼ lb [1.5 kg] floury potatoes, such as Maris Piper or russet
Scant ½ cup [100 g] butter
⅞ cup [200 ml] milk

For the filling
10½ oz [300 g] cod fillet, skinned
10½ oz [300 g] smoked haddock fillet, skinned
10½ oz [300 g] salmon fillet, skinned
4½ cups [1 L] whole milk
Scant ½ cup [100 g] butter
¾ cup [100 g] all-purpose flour
2 Tbsp finely diced shallots
2 Tbsp gherkins, chopped
1 Tbsp small capers in brine, drained and rinsed
2 Tbsp chopped parsley
1 Tbsp chopped tarragon
1 Tbsp chopped chives
1 Tbsp chopped chervil
Sea salt and freshly ground black pepper

For the topping
1½ packed cups [150 g] grated sharp Cheddar cheese
8 large eggs

For the mash, peel the potatoes, and cut into even-sized chunks. Place in a large pan, cover with cold water, add a large pinch of salt and bring to a boil. Reduce the heat, and simmer for about 20 minutes, until tender.

Drain the potatoes, and let them sit in the colander for a few minutes, then return to the pan. Mash until smooth, and beat in the butter and milk. Season well with salt and pepper, and set aside.

Preheat your oven to 350°F [180°C]. For the filling, pour the milk into a large pan and bring to a simmer. Meanwhile, cut all the fish into chunks.

Melt the butter in a medium pan over a fairly low heat, and stir in the flour. Cook, stirring, for a couple of minutes, being careful not to let it brown. Gradually stir in the hot milk. Bring to a boil, reduce the heat, and simmer for about 20 minutes. Take off the heat, and stir in the shallots, gherkins, capers, and herbs. Season the sauce with salt and pepper to taste. Add the fish, and toss to combine.

Transfer the seafood and sauce to a 12 in [30 cm] square (or similar) baking dish. Spoon or pipe the mashed potato on top, and scatter over the cheese. Bake for 20 minutes until the topping is golden.

Meanwhile, bring another pan of water to a boil, then carefully add the eggs. Cook for 6 minutes, then drain, and place under cold running water until the eggs are cool enough to handle. Peel the boiled eggs, and cut in half.

When the pie is ready, remove from the oven, and poke the halved boiled eggs into the potato topping. Serve immediately.

Great quality smoked haddock marries surprisingly well with curried lentils, and lime yogurt lends a cooling, refreshing contrast. If you're not keen on smoked fish, use plain haddock, hake, or cod— something with a good flake to it. And if you're not a fan of lentils, new potatoes work well.

Smoked haddock and curried lentils, lime yogurt

Serves 4 to 6

2 sides of smoked haddock, 18 to 21 oz [500 to 600 g] each, skinned and pin-boned
Scant ½ cup [100 g] unsalted butter, diced
3½ Tbsp light canola oil
Sea salt

For the curry paste

2 tsp coriander seeds
2 tsp cumin seeds
1 tsp fenugreek seeds
1 tsp yellow mustard seeds
4 garlic cloves, peeled
3 green chiles, halved and seeded

For the lentils

2 cups [400 g] Puy lentils
Light canola oil for cooking
2 red onions, peeled, and root removed, thinly sliced
Scant ½ cup [50 g] peeled and grated fresh ginger
2 garlic cloves, peeled and chopped
12 oz [350 g] baby plum tomatoes, halved
Scant ½ cup [100 ml] tamarind liquid (see note)
Scant ½ cup [100 ml] coconut milk
¼ cup [50 g] soft brown sugar
A handful of cilantro, leaves picked, and roughly chopped
A handful of mint, leaves picked, and roughly chopped

For the lime yogurt

Scant 1 cup [200 g] full-fat Greek yogurt
Finely grated zest and juice of 1 lime

Preheat your oven to 400°F [200°C].

Oil a sheet of aluminum foil large enough to hold the smoked haddock in one layer. Dot the butter over the fish, and then cover with another sheet of foil. Fold the edges together to form a sealed package, and place on a baking sheet. Bake for 15 minutes, then remove from the oven, and set the sealed package aside for 10 minutes to rest.

Meanwhile, for the curry paste, finely grind all the spices together in a spice grinder or with a mortar and pestle. Transfer to a small food processor, add the garlic and chiles, and whiz to a fine paste, adding a few drops of water if needed. Season with a good pinch of salt.

To cook the lentils, put them into a pan, add water to cover and some salt. Bring to a simmer over medium heat, and allow to simmer for 10 to 15 minutes until just cooked. Drain and transfer to a tray to cool.

Heat a sauté pan and add a drizzle of oil. Add the onions, ginger, and garlic, and sweat for 2 minutes, until starting to soften and color. Add the curry paste, and cook, stirring, for 2 minutes. Add the tomatoes, and cook for 3 minutes, until they start to break down. Add the tamarind liquid, coconut milk, and sugar. Bring to a simmer, and cook for 10 minutes.

For the yogurt, in a bowl mix the yogurt with the lime zest and juice, and season with salt to taste.

Unwrap the package and flake the fish into a bowl, keeping it in chunky flakes. Reserve the cooking juices.

When ready to serve, add the lentils to the sauce, and warm through for 2 minutes. Add half the herbs, the smoked haddock, and reserved cooking juices, and stir through carefully, trying not to break up the haddock flakes. Divide the curry between warmed bowls. Top with a generous spoonful of the lime yogurt, and scatter over the remaining herbs.

Note To make tamarind liquid, soak a piece about ¾-by-1¼-by-⅜-in [25 g] of compressed block tamarind in ⅔ cup [150 ml] warm water for 10 minutes, then strain through a fine strainer; discard the pulp.

Pasta bakes can be boring, but not this one! It's a fantastic way of using crab, especially as you include the tasty brown meat. Rice-shaped orzo pasta is particularly good here, but other pasta works too (see note). I use the best Cornish crab I can get my mitts on, but crab from anywhere is fine, so long as it's fresh. A shaved fennel and arugula salad tossed with a lemony dressing is a great accompaniment, as it cuts the richness perfectly.

Crab and saffron pasta bake

Serves 4

5¼ oz [150 g] brown crabmeat
7 oz [200 g] white crabmeat, picked
2¼ cups [300 g] orzo pasta
⅞ cup [200 ml] fish stock (see page 218)
⅔ cup [150 ml] milk
1¼ cups [300 ml] heavy cream
1 tsp saffron strands
½ cup [35 g] brown bread crumbs
⅓ cup [30 g] grated sharp Cheddar cheese

Preheat your oven to 350°F [180°C].

Bring a pan of salted water to a boil, and add the pasta. Bring back to a boil and cook for 6 to 7 minutes, then drain. Rinse out the pan, then return the pasta to it. Add the fish stock, milk, cream, and saffron. Bring to a boil, stirring all the time.

Add the brown crabmeat to the mixture, and immediately turn off the heat. Stir well, then add the white crabmeat. Stir again, then transfer the mixture to an oven dish.

Mix the bread crumbs and grated cheese together, and sprinkle over the pasta. Bake for 20 to 25 minutes, until golden and bubbling.

Note You can use any shaped pasta, but you'll need to adjust the initial cooking time accordingly—the aim is to undercook the pasta by a couple of minutes at this stage.

This is real comfort food for me. It's the sort of dish I want on a chilly spring evening, with plenty of good crusty bread to mop up the juices. It doesn't need anything else. You might like to add some extra smoked fish, such as mackerel or haddock, with the salmon. You could also bake small portions in little individual baking dishes to serve as an appetizer.

Smoked salmon, cauliflower, and asparagus bake

Serves 4

7 oz [200 g] smoked salmon
3½ Tbsp unsalted butter
6 Tbsp all-purpose flour
⅞ cup [200 ml] fish stock (see page 218)
⅞ cup [200 ml] whole milk
12 asparagus spears, woody parts removed, cut in half
1 large cauliflower, broken into small florets
2 tsp English mustard
2 Tbsp chopped parsley
1 Tbsp chopped tarragon
1 heaping cup [100 g] grated sharp Cheddar cheese
Sea salt and freshly ground black pepper

Preheat your oven to 400°F [200°C]. Cut the smoked salmon into strips and set aside.

To make the sauce, melt the butter in a saucepan, add the flour, and cook, stirring, for 3 minutes to make a roux. Heat the fish stock and milk together, and add to the pan gradually, little by little, stirring all the time to avoid lumps. Once all the liquid is incorporated, cook the sauce over low heat for 20 minutes, stirring every couple of minutes.

Meanwhile, bring a pan of salted water to a boil. Add the asparagus, and blanch for 2 minutes. Remove with a slotted spoon, and immediately plunge into a bowl of ice water to cool quickly. Blanch the cauliflower for 4 minutes and refresh in the same way.

When the vegetables are cold, drain well, and arrange in an oven dish. Lay the smoked salmon over and in between the vegetables.

When the sauce is ready, stir in the mustard and chopped herbs. Season with salt and pepper to taste. Pour the sauce over the vegetables and scatter the grated cheese on top. Bake for 15 minutes until golden and bubbling. Serve on warmed plates, with bread and butter on the side.

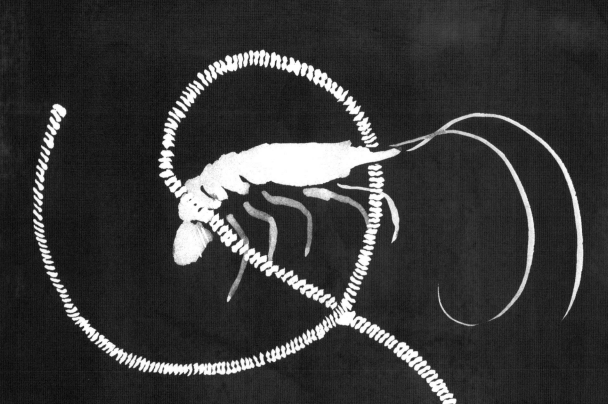
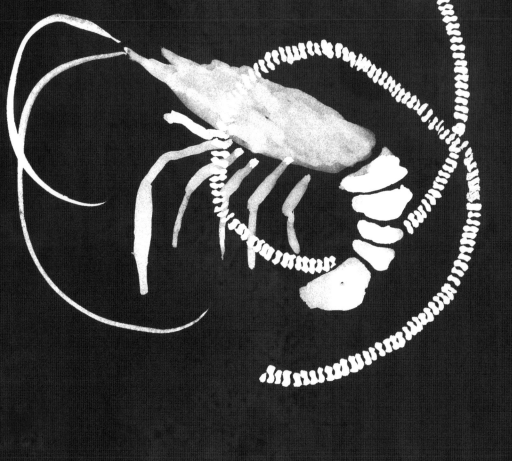

BROIL & BARBECUE

Broiling langoustines topped with a savory butter is one of the best ways to cook them in my view. All piled up on a plate, they look so inviting. The butter also works well with lobster, scallops, jumbo shrimp, or whole broiled English sole or lemon sole.

Langoustines with saffron and olive butter

Serves 4

20 whole raw langoustines, shell on, live or frozen

For the saffron and olive butter

½ tsp saffron strands
Finely grated zest and juice of 1 lemon
9 oz [250 g] unsalted butter, softened
1 shallot, peeled and chopped
1 garlic clove, peeled and chopped
2 Tbsp pitted black olives, chopped
20 basil leaves, finely sliced
Sea salt

To serve

2 lemons, halved

Place the langoustines on a board. Split them in half lengthwise from head to tail and remove the stomach and dark intestinal tract. Crack the claws and set aside.

To make the flavored butter, put the saffron and lemon juice into a small pan, and heat gently to infuse and encourage the saffron color to bleed out.

Put the butter, shallot, garlic, olives, basil, and lemon zest into a bowl and mix thoroughly until evenly blended. Spoon the butter onto a sheet of plastic wrap, wrap it up, and shape into a cylinder, about 1¼ in [3 cm] in diameter. Tie the ends to secure, and chill until ready to use. (The butter can be prepared ahead and frozen at this stage.)

Preheat your broiler to high. Meanwhile, cut the butter into thin discs (you'll need 40 in total). Place the 4 lemon halves, cut-side up, on a broiler pan and broil until they start to color.

Add the langoustines to the broiler pan, flesh-side uppermost, with the claws. Place a disc of butter on each langoustine half and broil for 4 to 5 minutes until the langoustines are cooked, and the lemon halves are tinged with brown, basting the langoustines with the melting butter occasionally.

Divide the langoustines between warmed bowls. Add the lemon halves and serve immediately.

Angels on horseback are typically served as a classic hors d'oeuvre or canapé. In the summer, I like to cook them on the barbecue, and serve them with a glass of bubbles or, I think, even better, a beer. I use our farmed Cornish rock oysters for this dish; I wouldn't use a Cornish native oyster for cooking. The pea pâté is really refreshing with the salty oyster and bacon, and it also makes a great vegetarian course on its own with some sourdough.

Angels on horseback, pea pâté

Serves 4
20 oysters, shucked
20 slices of smoked bacon
A drizzle of olive oil

For the pea pâté
2 cups [300 g] freshly podded
   or frozen peas
Scant ½ cup [100 g] full-fat
   cream cheese
Scant ½ cup [100 g] full-fat
   Greek yogurt
Juice of 1 lime
20 mint leaves, shredded
Sea salt and freshly ground
   black pepper

To finish
Extra virgin olive oil

To make the pea pâté, bring a pan of salted water to a boil, and have a bowl of ice water ready. Once the water is boiling, add the peas, and cook for 2 minutes. Drain, and then plunge the peas into the ice water to cool quickly, so they keep their color. When cold, drain well.

Transfer the peas to a food processor, and add the cream cheese, yogurt, lime juice, and mint. Blend for 3 minutes until smooth, then season with salt and pepper to taste. Spoon the pâté into a serving bowl, cover, and place in the fridge to set.

Light the barbecue about 30 minutes before you want to cook the oysters, or preheat the broiler. Meanwhile, check the oysters for any fragments of shell. Lay a slice of bacon on a board, place an oyster at one end and roll up to enclose the oyster. Thread onto a skewer to hold it together. Repeat with the rest of the oysters, threading 5 wrapped oysters onto each of 4 skewers.

To cook, drizzle the oysters with a little olive oil, and then carefully place them on the barbecue grid or broiler pan. Cook for 2 minutes on each side.

Once cooked, place the skewered oysters on a platter. Add a drizzle of olive oil to the pea pâté, and serve with the skewers.

This is a fun dish to serve as a warm canapé or appetizer. I really like the way oysters—and their shells—give off an amazing aroma of the sea when you broil them. The smoked hollandaise is down to the genius of my head chef, Chris Simpson. I've also cooked these oysters on a barbecue—the additional smoke works wonders, so give it a go if you get the chance. Scallops in the shell, and half lobsters are also great served this way.

Oysters with smoked hollandaise sauce

Serves 4 as an appetizer

12 live oysters
About 14 oz [400 g] rock salt
  for broiling, plus extra to
  serve
1 lemon, peeled, pith removed
  and cut into sections

**For the smoked hollandaise
  sauce**
9 oz [250 g] smoked butter
3 egg yolks
Juice of ½ lemon
Cayenne pepper, to taste
Sea salt
Dill leaves, minced,
  to finish

Open the oysters and prise off the top shell. Drain off the juices. Cut the muscle to release the oyster, but leave it in the rounded shell; check for any fragments of shell.

Preheat your broiler to its highest setting and line a broiler pan with enough salt to sit the oysters on to hold them steady. (If you don't have enough salt, make small aluminum foil rings to support the oyster shells.)

To make the hollandaise, melt the smoked butter in a pan over medium heat until it begins to bubble, then remove from the heat, and leave to cool until lukewarm. Meanwhile, put the egg yolks and lemon juice in a heatproof bowl over a pan of hot water set over medium-low heat, making sure the base of the bowl is not touching the water. Whisk until the mixture thickens enough to form ribbons when you lift the beaters.

Remove the bowl from the pan, and slowly whisk in the melted butter. Once it is all incorporated, season the hollandaise with cayenne pepper and salt. Taste and adjust the seasoning as necessary, adding a little more lemon juice too, if you think it is needed. Keep warm while you broil the oysters.

Lay the oysters in their shells on the prepared pan, and place under the broiler for 3 minutes. Remove from the broiler. Place a lemon section on each oyster and then spoon on some hollandaise. Put back under the broiler for a minute or so, until the hollandaise is just starting to brown.

Finish with a sprinkling of chopped dill, and a little more cayenne pepper. Serve immediately, on a bed of salt.

Recently, as I was eating lobster, its amazing smell mingled with the aroma of spices cooking in the kitchen and took me back to a once-in-a-lifetime family holiday in Jamaica, when I was twelve. I wanted to create something like the Jamaican dishes I enjoyed all those years ago. The lobsters we get in the UK and US are very different from the spiny lobsters of the Caribbean. I've toned down the heat and spice to allow the special flavors of our lobsters to come through, but if spice is your thing, feel free to add more!

Barbecued jerk lobster with coconut rice

Serves 2

2 live lobsters, 1¼ to 1¾ lb
[600 to 800 g] each

For the jerk sauce
A drizzle of sunflower oil
2 garlic cloves, peeled and
chopped
2 tsp chopped fresh ginger
1 bunch of scallions, finely
sliced
1 red chile, seeded and chopped
½ tsp ground cinnamon
½ tsp freshly grated nutmeg
½ tsp ground allspice
1 tsp chopped rosemary
1 bay leaf
Zest and juice of 1 lime
Zest and juice of 1 orange
¼ cup [50 g] superfine sugar
2 Tbsp dark soy sauce
⅞ cup [200 ml] chicken stock
(see page 218)
1 Tbsp chopped cilantro leaves
Sea salt

For the coconut rice
Heaping ¾ cup [140 g] basmati
rice
A drizzle of sunflower oil
4 scallions, finely sliced
1 garlic clove, peeled and finely
sliced
Scant ½ cup [100 ml] coconut
milk
Scant ½ cup [100 ml] chicken
stock (or water)

To serve
2 limes, halved
Chopped cilantro

Put the lobsters in the freezer for an hour before cooking to sedate them. Wash the rice in several changes of water, then leave to soak in cold water for 30 minutes.

To make the sauce, heat a large pan over medium heat, then add the oil. When hot, add the garlic, ginger, scallions, and chile, and fry for 2 minutes. Add the spices, rosemary, bay leaf, and citrus zests, and cook for 2 minutes, then add the sugar, soy sauce, citrus juices, and stock. Bring to a simmer, and let bubble for about 5 minutes to reduce and thicken. Add a pinch of salt and the chopped cilantro. Set aside to cool.

To kill the lobsters, firmly insert the tip of a strong chef's knife into the cross on the head. Now carefully cut the lobsters in half lengthwise, from head to tail. Remove the stomach sac from the head, and the dark intestinal thread running along the length of the tail. Crack the claws. Lay the lobster halves on a tray and spoon half the jerk sauce over them. Leave to marinate for 30 minutes, while you light and heat up the barbecue.

Meanwhile, drain the rice. Heat a pan (with a tight-fitting lid) and add the oil. When it is hot, add the scallions and garlic, and sweat for 2 minutes. Add the rice, and cook, stirring, for 1 minute. Pour in the coconut milk and stock, and bring to a simmer. Turn the heat down low, put the lid on, and cook for 10 minutes. Take the pan off the heat and leave to stand, covered, for 5 minutes.

To cook the lobsters, when the barbecue coals are white-hot, place the lobster claws on the barbecue grid and cook for 3 to 4 minutes. Turn the lobster claws over and add the lobster tails, shell-side down, and the lime halves, cut-side down. Cook for 3 to 4 minutes, then turn the lobster tails over, and cook for an additional 2 minutes.

When the lobster is cooked, transfer to a warmed platter, and spoon on some more jerk sauce. Sprinkle with chopped cilantro, and add the lime halves. Fluff up the rice with a fork, and serve on the side.

Broil and barbecue

This octopus dish really hits the spot. I've taken one of my favorite Spanish dishes, *ajo blanco* (white gazpacho) and used it as a bread sauce for the charred octopus. The flavors are great together, so give it a go. If you can't get hold of octopus, large squid can be cooked in the same way, or, even quicker, small raw squid or scallops can be added straight to the barbecue or broiler.

Seared octopus, almond and sherry vinegar bread sauce

Serves 4

1 octopus (double sucker species), about 2¼ lb [1 kg] (defrosted if frozen)
Olive oil for cooking
4 shallots, peeled and chopped
5 garlic cloves, peeled and crushed
2 rosemary sprigs
Scant ½ cup [100 ml] fino or other dry sherry
Finely grated zest of 1 lemon
Sea salt and freshly ground black pepper

For the almond and sherry vinegar bread sauce
¾ cup [100 g] whole almonds, blanched and skinned
4 slices [120 g] good crustless white or wholegrain bread, in chunks
2 garlic cloves, peeled and minced
6 Tbsp sherry vinegar
1¼ cups [300 ml] extra virgin olive oil

To garnish
A bunch of watercress, leaves picked
A small bunch of seedless green grapes, sliced
2 Tbsp chopped parsley
1 Tbsp chopped chives
Olive oil to drizzle

First you need to braise the octopus to tenderize it. Heat a pan large enough to hold the octopus (with a tight-fitting lid) and add a drizzle of olive oil. When hot, add the shallots, garlic, and rosemary. Cook for 2 minutes, then add the sherry, followed by the octopus and lemon zest. Put the lid on and cook gently for 1 hour, or until the octopus is tender.

In the meantime, make the bread sauce. Preheat your oven to 375°F [190°C]. Scatter the almonds on a baking sheet, and roast in the oven for 5 minutes. Put the bread into a bowl, add water to cover, and leave to soak for 5 to 10 minutes. Put the roasted almonds and garlic into a food processor, and pulse until smooth. Squeeze the bread to remove all excess water, then add to the food processor with a good pinch of salt. With the motor running, add the sherry vinegar, followed by the olive oil in a steady stream. Once all the oil is incorporated, taste and add more salt and vinegar if you like. Refrigerate until needed.

When the octopus is cooked, lift it out onto a tray and leave until cool enough to handle. Cut off and reserve the tentacles, discarding the beak. Slit open the main body and remove the ink sac, stomach, and eyes carefully. Cut the body meat into 4 equal pieces. Skewer these and the tentacles in portions. Oil the octopus, and season with salt and pepper, then set aside until ready to cook.

Light the barbecue about 30 minutes before you want to cook, or preheat the broiler. When the coals are white-hot or the broiler is ready, carefully place the octopus skewers on the barbecue grid or broiler pan and cook for 2 to 3 minutes on each side, until nicely colored and charred.

To serve, share the watercress and octopus between 4 plates. Toss the sliced grapes and chopped herbs together with a drizzle of olive oil and a little salt, then spoon over and around the octopus. Put a spoonful of bread sauce on each plate. Serve hot or cold.

The flavor that smoking coals give langoustines is quite something, and cannot be re-created with any other cooking method. You just need to be careful as you turn or handle the langoustines, as they are quite fragile. The tomato and chili chutney is a great accompaniment; if you have any left, it will keep in the fridge for a few weeks. Large raw shrimp and lobster are also excellent cooked this way.

Barbecued langoustines with tomato and chile chutney

Serves 4

16 medium or large raw langoustines, shell on, live or frozen

For the seasoning
1 tsp coriander seeds
2 tsp salt
Finely grated zest of 2 lemons
1 tsp dried oregano

For the tomato chutney
Olive oil for cooking
2 red onions, peeled and minced
2 tsp coriander seeds
4 garlic cloves, peeled and minced
8 red chiles, seeded and minced
¾ cup [100 g] peeled and finely grated fresh ginger,
Generous 1½ lb [700 g] ripe plum tomatoes, blanched, skinned and chopped
1 cup [200 g] dark brown sugar
Scant ½ cup [100 ml] red wine vinegar
3½ Tbsp [50 ml] balsamic vinegar
2 tsp salt

To make the chutney, heat a large saucepan over medium heat, and add a drizzle of olive oil. When hot, add the onions with the coriander seeds, and cook for 6 to 8 minutes, until the onions are softened and just starting to brown. Add the garlic, chiles, and ginger, and cook for 4 minutes. Now add the tomatoes, sugar, both vinegars, and the salt. Cook, stirring occasionally, for 20 minutes, until the mixture is well-reduced and sticky; it will start to stick on the bottom of the pan. Remove from the heat.

Using a stick blender, blitz the chutney briefly to break it up a bit, but don't go too far—it should have some texture. Taste for seasoning, and add more salt if you think it needs it. Transfer the chutney to a bowl, and allow to cool, then refrigerate.

To prepare the seasoning for the langoustines, toast the coriander seeds in a dry pan over medium heat for a minute or two until fragrant, then remove from the heat, and add the salt, lemon zest, and oregano. Using a mortar and pestle or spice grinder, grind the mixture until fine. Set aside.

Light your barbecue 30 minutes before you are planning to cook. Place the langoustines on a board. Split them in half lengthwise from head to tail, and remove the stomach and dark intestinal tract. Crack the claws, and set aside.

Once the coals are white-hot, sprinkle the langoustines all over with the prepared seasoning, and place them on the barbecue grid, cut-side down. Cook for 2 minutes, then carefully turn them over and cook for an additional 2 minutes.

To serve, place the langoustines on a large platter with a pot of the chutney, and let everyone help themselves.

I think lemon sole are one of the most underrated fish. When they are at their best, between February and May, they are magnificent broiled whole. A zesty herb butter, flavored with capers and anchovies is the perfect complement. All you need is some minted new potatoes on the side.

Lemon sole, green sauce butter

Serves 4

4 lemon sole, 18 to 25 oz
  [500 to 700 g] each
Olive oil for cooking
Sea salt and freshly ground
  black pepper

For the green sauce butter
1 shallot, peeled and minced
1 garlic clove, peeled, halved
  (germ removed) and
  chopped
2 Tbsp chopped flat-leaf
  parsley
2 Tbsp chopped arugula
  leaves
1 Tbsp chopped mint
1 Tbsp chopped basil
2 anchovy fillets in oil,
  drained and chopped
1 tsp small capers in brine,
  drained, rinsed and chopped
½ tsp English mustard
Finely grated zest and juice
  of ½ lemon
10½ oz [300 g] unsalted
  butter, softened

For the garnish
1¼ cups [300 ml] sunflower
  oil for deep-frying
2 Tbsp large capers, drained,
  rinsed and chopped

For the green sauce butter, put all the chopped ingredients into a bowl with the English mustard, lemon zest, and juice. Add the softened butter, and mix thoroughly until evenly blended. Season with salt and pepper to taste. Spoon the butter onto a sheet of plastic wrap, wrap it in the plastic wrap, and shape into a cylinder. Tie the ends to secure, and chill until ready to use. (The butter can be prepared ahead, and frozen at this stage.)

For the garnish, heat the sunflower oil in a small, deep, heavy pan over medium heat to 350°F [180°C]. Add the capers, and fry for 1 minute until crispy. Remove with a slotted spoon, and drain on paper towels; keep warm.

Preheat your broiler to high. Oil a broiler pan large enough to comfortably hold the fish (or cook them two at a time). Oil the fish, season all over with salt and pepper, and place on the broiler pan, dark side up. Cut the butter into discs and lay on top of the fish.

Cook the sole under the broiler for 10 to 12 minutes. To check for doneness, insert a small knife into the thickest part of the fish, near the head, and pull at the bone. You should see the fillet coming away from the bone; if not, cook it for another couple of minutes or so until it does.

To serve, carefully lift the fish onto warmed plates and spoon over the butter, along with any cooking juices left on the broiler pan. Finish with the deep-fried capers, and serve immediately.

The sense of smell is amazing. When I cook this, the aroma takes me right back to 1999 when I was preparing a similar dish at Rick Stein's The Seafood Restaurant in Padstow. The smell of red mullet cooking is unlike any other fish—it is utterly unique. That, and the smell of the chanterelles pan-frying with garlic and parsley, is enough to bring any food lover to their knees.

Red mullet with chanterelles and roasted garlic aïoli

Serves 4

4 red mullet (goatfish), 18 to 21 oz [500 to 600 g] each, scaled, filleted, and pin-boned
Olive oil for broiling
Sea salt and freshly ground black pepper

For the roasted garlic aïoli
1 garlic bulb
2 egg yolks
Finely grated zest and juice of 1 lemon
1¾ cups [400 ml] olive oil

For the chanterelles
14 oz [400 g] chanterelles, cleaned and halved or quartered if large
A drizzle of olive oil
Scant ½ cup [100 g] unsalted butter
2 shallots, peeled and chopped
1 garlic clove, peeled and minced
⅓ cup [75 ml] sherry vinegar
3 Tbsp chopped flat-leaf parsley

Preheat your oven to 400°F [200°C]. For the roasted garlic, wrap the garlic bulb in some aluminum foil, place it in an oven dish, and bake for 45 minutes until soft. Unwrap the garlic, and leave until cool enough to handle. Separate the cloves and squeeze out the soft garlic pulp.

To make the aïoli, put the egg yolks, lemon zest and juice, and the roasted garlic pulp into a small food processor. Blend briefly to combine, then, with the motor running, slowly add the olive oil in a thin, steady stream through the funnel until it is all incorporated, and the sauce is emulsified. Season with salt and pepper, blend for an additional 30 seconds, then taste and adjust the seasoning if necessary. Transfer to a bowl, cover, and refrigerate until ready to serve.

Preheat your broiler to its highest setting.

To cook the chanterelles, heat a large skillet over medium heat, then add the olive oil and butter. When bubbling, add the chanterelles and fry for 2 minutes.

At the same time, brush the red mullet (goatfish) fillets with oil, season them, and place skin-side up under the broiler.

Now add the shallots and garlic to the chanterelles, cook for another minute, then add the sherry vinegar. Toss in the parsley, season with salt and pepper, and remove from the heat.

By now, your red mullet fillets will be coloring and almost ready—they will take about 4 minutes. To check, lift one up carefully, and turn it over. The flesh should be white with no sign of rawness.

Place a large spoonful of the roasted garlic aïoli in the middle of each warmed plate and add a red mullet fillet. Share the chanterelles between the plates, and serve immediately.

This is a really nice dish for late summer when bass is great, zucchini are aplenty, and herbs are thriving. The lovely saltiness of the air-dried ham (prosciutto or Bayonne), with the zingy lemon and fresh herbs, works brilliantly with the bass. If the weather's good, you could barbecue the bass whole, and just serve it with the zucchini salad and dressing.

Bass with air-dried ham, zucchini, lemon, and herbs

Serves 4

1 bass, 3¼ to 4½ lb [1.5 to 2 kg], gutted, scaled, filleted, and pin-boned
2 Tbsp olive oil, plus extra to drizzle and dress the zucchini
1 white onion, peeled and diced
3 garlic cloves, peeled, halved (germ removed) and sliced
8 slices of air-dried ham, cut into strips
1¼ cups [300 ml] fish stock (see page 218)
1 cup [250 ml] heavy cream
3 zucchini
1 Tbsp chopped tarragon
1 Tbsp chopped flat-leaf parsley
1 Tbsp chopped dill
1 Tbsp chopped chives
Finely grated zest and juice of 1 lemon
2 Tbsp Dijon mustard
Sea salt and freshly ground black pepper

To make the sauce, heat a medium pan over medium heat, and add the 2 Tbsp olive oil. When it is hot, add the onion and garlic, and cook for 3 minutes to soften. Add the ham, and cook for an additional 4 minutes, until it is starting to crisp.

Pour in the fish stock, bring to a simmer, and let bubble until reduced by half. Add the cream, bring back to a simmer, and cook for 10 minutes, until the sauce starts to thicken.

Meanwhile finely slice the zucchini lengthwise, on a mandoline if you have one (or veg peeler if not), and place in a bowl. Add the herbs, with half of the lemon zest and juice. Drizzle with olive oil, season with salt and pepper, and toss well.

Preheat your broiler to high.

To finish the sauce, add the remaining lemon juice and mustard, and season with a little salt and pepper. Bring to a simmer, then taste and adjust the seasoning. Set aside while you cook the fish.

Cut the bass fillets in half to give 4 equal portions, and place skin-side up on a broiler pan. Drizzle with olive oil, sprinkle on the remaining lemon zest, and season with salt and pepper. Broil the fish for 5 to 7 minutes.

Meanwhile, give the zucchini another toss and then drain in a colander set over a bowl to collect the dressing. Remove the fish from the broiler, and leave to rest and finish cooking on the pan for 1 minute.

Spoon the sauce onto 4 warmed plates. Pile two-thirds of the zucchini in the center, and lay a portion of bass on top. Arrange the remaining zucchini ribbons on the fish, and finish with a spoonful or two of the dressing. Serve immediately.

If it's warm enough for a barbecue, I always look out for fresh sardines, as they are amazing cooked over coals. The pepper salad goes perfectly, and I love the fact that you can use the barbecue for that too. If you fancy it, you can add a few other veggies to the peppers as well, such as zucchini or mushrooms—I usually grab whatever is at hand. If you can't get sardines, mackerel is a great alternative. And if the weather's iffy, use the broiler instead.

Smoked paprika sardines, marinated pepper salad

Serves 4

12 fresh sardines, scaled and gutted
4 tsp sweet smoked paprika
2 tsp salt
About ½ scant cup [100 ml] olive oil

For the marinated pepper salad

2 red bell peppers
1 yellow bell pepper
1 green bell pepper
2 red onions, peeled and each cut into 6 wedges
3 garlic cloves, peeled and minced
2 thyme sprigs, leaves picked and chopped
20 basil leaves, finely sliced
Scant ½ cup [100 ml] red wine vinegar
Scant ½ cup [100 ml] extra virgin olive oil
A couple of handfuls of arugula leaves
Sea salt and freshly ground black pepper

To serve

2 lemons, halved

For the pepper salad, peel the skin from the peppers, using a vegetable peeler (don't worry if you don't get all the skin off). Halve, core, and seed the peppers, then cut into bite-sized pieces. Place in a bowl with the onion wedges, garlic, thyme, basil, wine vinegar, and olive oil. Season with salt and pepper, and leave to marinate for 15 to 20 minutes.

Light your barbecue about 30 minutes before you want to begin cooking (or preheat the broiler). When it is almost ready, thread the peppers and onions onto skewers. Reserve the oil and vinegar remaining in the bowl for the dressing.

When the barbecue coals are white-hot (or the broiler is ready), lay the vegetable skewers on the grid (or broiler pan) and cook for 6 to 8 minutes, turning occasionally, until the peppers are charred and soft. Slide the vegetables off the skewers into a bowl and set aside to cool.

Meanwhile, season the sardines with the smoked paprika and salt and drizzle all over with olive oil. Lay them on the barbecue grid or broiler pan and cook for 3 minutes on each side, turning carefully.

To serve, dress the peppers and onions with the reserved oil and vinegar mixture. Add the arugula leaves, and toss to combine. Serve the sardines with the pepper salad, lemon halves, and a sprinkling of salt.

Broil and barbecue

Monkfish marinated and cooked this way is particularly special. This fish really benefits from being cooked on the bone, as it helps to stop the flesh shrinking too much. It works well on the barbecue, but make sure you get the coals white-hot, or it will stick, and you'll lose some of the marinade as a result. The spiced butter dressing enhances the flavor perfectly.

Monkfish on the bone, spiced butter, and fennel

Serves 4

2¾ to 3¼ lb [1.2 to 1.5 kg] monkfish tail on the bone, trimmed of sinew and skin
Scant ½ cup [100 ml] sunflower oil
Finely grated zest of 2 lemons
½ tsp cayenne pepper
½ tsp freshly grated nutmeg
1 tender rosemary sprig, leaves picked and minced
Sea salt and freshly ground black pepper

For the spiced butter dressing

7 oz [200 g] unsalted butter
1 rosemary sprig
Finely grated zest and juice of 2 lemons
½ tsp cayenne pepper
½ tsp freshly grated nutmeg
4 shallots, peeled and chopped
2 large gherkins, minced
2 tsp small capers in brine, drained and rinsed
4 Tbsp chopped flat-leaf parsley

For the fennel

2 fennel bulbs, tough outer layer removed, cut into quarters
Olive oil to drizzle

Place the monkfish in a dish and add the oil, lemon zest, cayenne, nutmeg, rosemary, salt and pepper. Turn the fish to coat, cover with plastic wrap, and leave to marinate in the fridge for at least 2 (or up to 6) hours.

If you are barbecuing, light your barbecue at least 30 minutes before you plan to cook, or preheat the broiler.

For the spiced butter dressing, heat the butter and rosemary in a pan over medium heat, until the butter has melted, and begins to turn brown. Immediately take the pan off the heat, and add the lemon zest, cayenne, nutmeg, a pinch of salt, and the shallots. Remove the rosemary.

For the fennel, bring a large pan of salted water to a boil. Add the fennel, and cook for 6 to 8 minutes, until it starts to soften, but is still quite firm. Drain, and place on a tray to cool. Drizzle with olive oil and season.

When the coals are white-hot, or the broiler is ready, remove the monkfish from the marinade, and lay on the barbecue grid or broiler rack. Cook for 4 minutes, then turn the fish over, and cook for an additional 4 minutes. Remove, and set aside to rest on a warmed plate while you barbecue or broil the fennel for 5 minutes, turning to color as necessary.

Meanwhile, finish the dressing. Put the lemon juice, gherkins, capers, and chopped parsley into a small pan and add any cooking juices from the broiler pan. Now add the spiced butter, and give the dressing a good stir. Taste, and adjust the seasoning. Heat the dressing until it is just too hot to hold your finger in it, then remove from the heat.

To serve, briefly put the monkfish back on the barbecue or under the broiler to warm through for a couple of minutes. Place the fennel and the monkfish on a warmed platter, and spoon on the spiced butter dressing. Serve in the center of the table and let everyone help themselves.

Broil and barbecue

Monkfish is the perfect fish to cook on a grill or barbecue, because it can handle big flavors and has a firm texture that responds well to aggressive cooking. It's essential to make sure that whatever you are cooking the monkfish on, is red hot; if not it will stick, and you won't get a lovely charred finish to the outside. If you're using wooden skewers, pre-soak them in cold water for 30 minutes or so, to prevent them burning before the monkfish is cooked.

Monkfish satay

Serves 4

21 oz [600 g] monkfish fillet, trimmed of sinew and skin, cut into chunks
2 Tbsp coriander seeds
2 garlic cloves, peeled and minced
2 Tbsp finely grated fresh ginger
3 lemongrass stalks, coarse outer layers removed, minced
2 Tbsp sunflower oil
2 tsp soy sauce
2 tsp fish sauce
Grated zest of 1 lime (use the juice for the sauce)
Sea salt and freshly ground black pepper

For the peanut sauce

A drizzle of sunflower oil
6 shallots or 2 banana shallots, peeled and minced
4 garlic cloves, peeled and minced
2 red chiles, seeded and minced
2 Tbsp brown sugar
1 Tbsp fish sauce
⅞ cup [200 ml] coconut milk
1¼ cups [160 g] unsalted peanuts, roasted and finely chopped
Juice of 1 lime

To serve

1 lime, cut into quarters

For the marinade, toast the coriandeer seeds in a dry pan over medium heat for a minute or two, until fragrant. Using a mortar and pestle, or spice grinder, grind the seeds to a powder. Add the garlic, ginger, and lemongrass, and grind again. Add the oil, soy sauce, fish sauce, and lime zest and mix well.

Lay the monkfish chunks on a tray, and coat all over with the marinade. Cover the tray with plastic wrap, and refrigerate for 1 hour. If you are barbecuing, light your barbecue 30 minutes before you intend to cook.

Meanwhile, make the peanut sauce. Heat a medium pan over medium heat, then add the oil. When it is hot, add the shallots, garlic, and chiles, and sweat for 3 minutes. Stir in the sugar, and cook for an additional 3 minutes, then add the fish sauce and coconut milk. Bring to a boil, and let bubble for a couple of minutes. Stir in the peanuts and lime juice, then season with salt and pepper to taste. Keep warm (or allow to cool if preparing ahead and reheat to serve).

When the monkfish is ready, thread 4 to 5 chunks onto each of 4 skewers. If using a grill pan, heat up over high heat. When the grill pan is smoking, or the barbecue coals are white-hot, carefully lay the monkfish on the grill or grid, and cook for 2 minutes on each side.

Serve the monkfish on or off the skewers, with lime wedges and the peanut sauce in a bowl on the side. Accompany with plain rice, and a leafy side salad.

Broil and barbecue

Monkfish is probably the best fish to barbecue, but it does benefit from a little help flavorwise. Here I'm using Indian spices to give it a kick, and bring the fish alive. The spicy cauliflower pickle and refreshing ginger and cilantro yogurt, are ideal accompaniments.

Monkfish, cauliflower pickle, ginger and cilantro yogurt

Serves 4

4 monkfish tails on the bone, 7 to 10 oz [200 to 300 g] each, trimmed of sinew and skin
1 Tbsp mild curry powder
1 Tbsp cumin seeds
1 Tbsp coriander seeds
½ Tbsp sea salt

For the pickle
A drizzle of sunflower oil
1 small cauliflower, cut into florets
1 fennel bulb, tough outer layer removed, thinly sliced (ideally on a mandoline)
1 red onion, peeled and thinly sliced (ideally on a mandoline)
2 green chiles, halved, seeded and thinly sliced
⅞ cup [200 ml] white wine vinegar
1 tsp salt
1 tsp ground cumin
1 tsp ground coriander seeds
Canola oil to dress
2 Tbsp chopped cilantro

For the ginger and cilantro yogurt
1 cup [200 g] full-fat Greek yogurt
3 Tbsp ginger juice (see note)
2 Tbsp chopped cilantro
Salt

First, make the pickle. Heat a skillet over medium heat, and add the oil. When hot, add the cauliflower florets, and sweat for a few minutes without coloring, until they start to soften slightly. Add the fennel, onion, and chiles, and heat for a minute, then transfer to a bowl.

Put the wine vinegar, salt, and spices into a pan and bring to a boil, then strain the hot liquid over the cauliflower mixture. Cover the bowl with plastic wrap, and set aside to cool completely.

For the monkfish, toast the spices in a dry pan over medium heat for a minute until fragrant. Using a mortar and pestle or spice grinder, grind the toasted spices. Once the spice mix has cooled down, stir in the salt.

Coat the monkfish all over with the spice mixture, and leave to marinate in the fridge for at least 30 minutes and up to 3 hours.

For the yogurt, mix the yogurt, ginger juice, and chopped cilantro together in a bowl, and season with salt to taste. Cover and refrigerate until ready to serve.

If you are barbecuing, light your barbecue 30 minutes before you plan to cook, or preheat the broiler. When the coals are white-hot, or the broiler is ready, lay the monkfish tails on the barbecue grid or broiler rack, and cook for 4 to 5 minutes on each side, turning carefully.

Meanwhile, to finish the pickle, drain the cauliflower mixture, and return to the bowl. Dress with a generous glug of canola oil, and toss through the chopped cilantro. Season with salt to taste, and mix well.

Serve the fish with a generous spoonful of the cauliflower pickle, and the ginger and cilantro yogurt on the side.

Note To make the ginger juice, grate a heaping 1 cup [150 g] of freshly peeled ginger and squeeze tightly in a piece of cheesecloth over a bowl to extract the juice.

Hake deserves to be more popular. It's an excellent variety for coaxing non-fish eaters and children to eat fish, especially if you serve it this way. The lovely bacon, hazelnut, and earthy leek flavors merge as the fish cooks and the juices that collect in the broiler pan are amazing. You could make this dish with any member of the cod family.

Hake with bacon, hazelnuts, and leeks

Serves 4

4 filleted portions of hake, about 6½ oz [180 g] each, skin on
8 medium leeks, dark green part removed, well washed
8 slices of smoked bacon
¾ cup [100 g] blanched hazelnuts
Olive oil for cooking
Sea salt and freshly ground black pepper

For the dressing
1 shallot, peeled and minced
1 garlic clove, peeled, halved, (germ removed) and minced
1 Tbsp English mustard
3 Tbsp verjus or lemon juice
3 Tbsp water
1¾ cups [400 ml] light olive oil

To finish
2 Tbsp chopped flat-leaf parsley

To cook the leeks, bring a large pan of salted water to a boil over medium heat. Cut the leeks in half crosswise add to the pan, and cook for 12 minutes until tender (I like my leeks well-cooked, not *al dente*).

Preheat your broiler to medium. Season the hake portions with salt and pepper; set aside.

Lay the bacon on a broiler pan and cook for about 5 minutes until crispy, turning halfway. Save any bacon fat on the pan, to add to the dressing.

Drain the leeks thoroughly, and transfer to a shallow broilerproof dish (large enough to hold the leeks in a single layer). Leave to cool slightly.

To make the dressing, put the shallot, garlic, mustard, verjus or lemon juice, and water into a blender. Blend briefly to combine, then, with the motor running, slowly add the olive oil in a thin, steady stream through the funnel until it is all incorporated, and the dressing is emulsified. Add the retained bacon fat too. Pour the dressing over the leeks.

Scatter the hazelnuts on a broiler pan, and toast them under the broiler until golden all over, turning as necessary to color evenly. Transfer the nuts to a board, and chop them roughly. Do the same to the bacon. Sprinkle the bacon and nuts over the leeks.

Lay the hake portions on top of the leeks and place under the broiler. Cook for 6 to 8 minutes, depending on the thickness of the fish.

Either serve on a large warmed platter in the middle of the table and let everyone help themselves, or place on individual plates. Finish with a scattering of chopped parsley. I like this best with mashed potato, but it is also good with new potatoes.

I get asked quite often what my final meal would be, which is a bit concerning. I'd rather be asked what would be my favorite thing to eat. Barbecued mackerel straight out of the sea, and cooked on the beach has to be the answer. There's nothing quite like it: the freshness of the fish, the oiliness of the flesh and the blistering of the skin from the hot coals. Oh, and the lovely smokiness. The barbecue sauce is something of a classic in my kitchens. If you have any left, it will keep in a bottle in the fridge for up to a week, or you can freeze it.

Mackerel with barbecue sauce

Serves 4

4 large or 8 small mackerel, gutted

For the rub
2 tsp dried red pepper flakes
1 Tbsp fennel seeds
1 tsp black peppercorns
Grated zest of 2 oranges (use the juice for the sauce)
1 Tbsp sea salt
1 Tbsp chopped rosemary

For "my" barbecue sauce
A drizzle of olive oil
2 shallots, peeled and chopped
8 garlic cloves, peeled and chopped
3 green chiles, seeded and chopped
A bunch of tarragon, leaves picked and chopped
8 rosemary sprigs, leaves picked and chopped
A small bunch of parsley, leaves picked and chopped
3 Tbsp fennel seeds
Grated zest and juice of 2 oranges
½ cup [100 g] soft brown sugar
⅔ cup [150 ml] red wine vinegar
⅞ cup [200 ml] freshly squeezed orange juice
1 Tbsp English mustard
14 oz [400 g] good quality canned plum tomatoes
Sea salt and freshly ground black pepper

To prepare the rub, toast the spices in a dry pan over medium heat for a minute or so until fragrant, and starting to crackle a bit. Add the orange zest, salt, and rosemary and heat for 30 seconds. Tip the contents of the pan into a mortar, and grind with the pestle until fine. Leave to cool.

Slash the skin of the mackerel 3 or 4 times on each side and place the fish on a tray. Sprinkle all over with the spice mixture, and rub it into the slashes. Leave to marinate in the fridge for 1 hour.

To make the barbecue sauce, heat a sauté pan over medium heat, and add the olive oil. When hot, add the shallots, garlic, and chiles, and sweat for 3 minutes. Stir in the chopped herbs, fennel seeds, and orange zest, and cook for another minute. Add the sugar and wine vinegar, and stir until the sugar is dissolved, then let bubble to reduce until syrupy.

Add the orange juice, mustard, and tomatoes with their juice. Bring to a simmer, and let bubble until the liquid has reduced by half. Taste, then season with salt and pepper as required.

Transfer the contents of the pan to a food processor and blitz for 3 minutes. Strain the sauce through a strainer into a bowl, and leave to cool.

Light your barbecue 30 minutes before you plan on eating. When the coals are white-hot, place the mackerel on the barbecue grid. Cook for 3 minutes on one side, then carefully turn the fish over, and cook on the other side for 3 minutes. (Alternatively, you can cook the mackerel under a hot broiler.)

Carefully lift the fish onto a serving platter, using a big fish spatula, not tongs—mackerel is too delicate for these. Serve immediately, with my barbecue sauce on the side.

Broil and barbecue

On a visit to the Basque region of Spain, I sat outside a fantastic restaurant in Getaria, and watched huge turbots being cooked on a magnificent barbecue. The taste was something else, and I was determined to try and re-create the dish when I got home. Cooking a whole turbot is something you should have a go at; I know it's not cheap, but it will be worth every penny, I promise. The potatoes are a simple Basque staple.

Turbot "Getaria", Basque potatoes

Serves 6

1 turbot, about 6½ lb [3 kg]
2⅛ cups [500 ml] olive oil
1¼ cups [300 ml] white wine vinegar
Sea salt and freshly ground black pepper

For the Basque potatoes

3 large potatoes, peeled and sliced
Olive oil for cooking
1 white onion, peeled and chopped
2 garlic cloves, peeled and chopped
2 red bell peppers, peeled, cored, seeded, and sliced
2⅛ cups [500 ml] hot chicken stock (see page 218)
2 Tbsp chopped flat-leaf parsley

For the potatoes, preheat your oven to 350°F [180°C]. Heat a skillet large enough to take all the potatoes (or use two pans) over medium-high heat, then add a drizzle of olive oil. When hot, add the onion, garlic, and red bell peppers, and fry for 4 to 5 minutes until starting to brown. Add the potato slices, and fry for 2 minutes, adding a little more oil if needed.

Transfer the contents of the pan to an oven dish, pour on the hot chicken stock, and season with salt and pepper. Bake for 30 minutes, or until the potatoes are tender.

In the meantime, light the barbecue 30 minutes before you plan to cook the fish.

Combine the olive oil and wine vinegar in a bottle or jar, and give it a good shake.

When the coals are white-hot, season the fish liberally with salt, and place it in a large fish grilling basket. Put the fish on the barbecue, and cook for a total of 15 minutes, turning and basting with the oil and vinegar mix every 2 to 3 minutes.

When the fish is nearly cooked, remove from the heat and allow it to rest for 10 minutes before eating. Serve the turbot whole, on a warmed platter, with the potatoes on the side.

Sea robin are fantastic for the barbecue. They love a good marinade, and can handle bold flavors. I like to cook the small red species, but the bigger grey or tub sea robin is just as good. Try to avoid those with scales that seem impossible to remove—they are very sharp. The fennel salad is a lovely accompaniment, but you can serve what you like with the barbecued fish—or just eat them on their own with a squeeze of lemon, as I often do. Eating fish in this way allows you to really appreciate the difference between species, textures, and tastes.

Sea robin with fennel, gherkin, and olive salad

Serves 4

4 sea robin, 12 to 14 oz [350 to 400 g] each
Sea salt and freshly ground black pepper

For the marinade
4 tsp fennel seeds
2 garlic cloves, peeled and minced
4 tsp chopped thyme
2 tsp salt
Scant ½ cup [100 ml] olive oil

For the fennel, gherkin and olive salad
2 banana shallots, peeled and thinly sliced
Finely grated zest and juice of 1 lemon
3 large gherkins, sliced
2 fennel bulbs, tough outer layer removed
1 cup [100 g] pitted and sliced black olives
2 Tbsp fennel fronds, roughly torn
Scant ½ cup [100 ml] olive oil

For the marinade, toast the fennel seeds in a hot, dry pan for a couple of minutes until fragrant, then transfer to a mortar and grind finely with the pestle. Add the garlic, thyme, and salt and grind to a paste. Add the olive oil and mix well.

Score the sea robin several times on each side and rub all over with the marinade—be careful of the sharp bits! Leave to marinate in the fridge for at least an hour. Light your barbecue 30 minutes before you plan to start cooking, or preheat the broiler to high.

To prepare the salad, put the shallots in a bowl with the lemon juice, sliced gherkins, and a good pinch of salt. Toss to mix, and leave to stand for 10 minutes.

Meanwhile, thinly slice the fennel, using a mandoline if you have one. Add the fennel, olives, lemon zest and fennel fronds to the shallot mix and toss well. Dress with the olive oil. Taste for seasoning, adding more salt and a little pepper if you like.

When the coals are white-hot, or the broiler is ready, scrape off most of the marinade from the sea robin, and carefully lay the fish on the barbecue grid or broiler pan. Cook for 4 minutes on one side, then carefully turn the fish using a fish spatula and cook for an additional 4 minutes.

When the fish are cooked, carefully lift them onto a large platter. Serve immediately, with the salad on the side.

Broil and barbecue

TO
FOLLOW

More like a French financier or madeleine than a traditional sponge, this is a versatile recipe that can take all manner of spices and pretty much any fruit. Rhubarb is one of my favorite fruits to bake, and is delicious with the almond cream and sponge. All that richness and nuttiness is brought back to earth with the zingy crème fraîche. I like to serve these desserts warm from the oven, but you can let them cool down before eating if you prefer.

Rhubarb sponge, almond cream, and lemon crème fraîche

Serves 8

For the sponge
2 vanilla beans, split
  lengthwise
8 oz [225 g] unsalted butter
1 cup [225 g] egg whites (5 to
  6 extra large)
1⅛ cups [225 g] superfine
  sugar
⅞ cup [90 g] ground almonds
⅔ cup [90 g] all-purpose flour
8 pieces of rhubarb, about
  4 in [10 cm] long

For the almond cream
⅞ cup [90 g] ground almonds
⅓ cup [65 g] superfine sugar
1¼ cups [300 ml] whole milk
1 vanilla bean, split
  lengthwise

For the baked rhubarb
2¼ lb [1 kg] rhubarb, cut into
  3 to 4 in [8 to 10 cm] pieces
1¼ cups [250 g] superfine
  sugar
Zest and juice of 1 orange
  (zest microplaned)
Scant ½ cup [100 ml] water

For the lemon crème fraîche
2½ cups [600 ml] full-fat
  crème fraîche
¾ cup [100 g] confectioners'
  sugar
Grated zest and juice of
  1 lemon

Preheat your oven to 400°F [200°C]. Line 8 individual molds, about 3¼-by-1½-in [8-by-4 cm], with baking parchment.

To make the sponge, scrape the seeds from the vanilla beans and set aside. Put the beans into a saucepan with the butter, and place over medium heat. When the butter has melted and starts to brown, remove from the heat and allow to cool, then discard the vanilla beans.

Meanwhile, make the almond cream. Put the ground almonds, sugar, and milk into a heavy-bottomed pan with the vanilla. Place over medium heat and cook, stirring often, until thickened; this will take about 15 minutes.

In the meantime, bake the rhubarb. Put the rhubarb, sugar, orange zest and juice, and the water into a deep roasting pan. Cook in the oven until the rhubarb is soft, about 10 minutes. Remove from the oven, and leave to cool in the liquid.

When the almond cream is ready, remove from the heat, discard the vanilla bean, and cover the surface with plastic wrap to stop a skin forming.

To make the sponge, whisk the egg whites and sugar together in a large bowl for 1 minute. Add the ground almonds, flour, and vanilla seeds, and mix well. Finally, whisk in the brown butter, ensuring it is all incorporated. Pour the mixture into the prepared molds. Lay the 8 rhubarb pieces on top of the mixture and bake for 12 to 14 minutes.

For the lemon crème fraîche, whisk the crème fraîche, confectioners' sugar, lemon zest and juice together in a bowl. Cover, and refrigerate until needed.

To check if the sponges are baked, insert a small knife into the center of one; if it comes out clean, it is ready. Turn out the sponges, and place in shallow bowls. Serve warm with the baked rhubarb, almond cream, and lemon crème fraîche.

Crumble has got to be one of the all-time favorite British desserts. All that crunchy, slightly chewy topping with wonderful seasonal fruit underneath, served with lashings of custard, cream, or ice cream—you can't go wrong... as long as you can make a good one. I like to cook this in individual dishes, but you can make a big crumble if you prefer. Any leftovers will reheat well too—I've even been known to have it for breakfast!

Pear crumble with Earl Grey chocolate sauce

Serves 4

For roasting
4 pears

For the pear compote
8 pears
¼ cup [50 g] unsalted butter
Scant ½ cup [100 ml] hard pear cider
2 vanilla beans, split lengthwise, and seeds scraped

For the crumble mix
¾ cup [100 g] all-purpose flour
1½ cups [150 g] ground almonds
½ cup [100 g] golden superfine sugar
½ cup [100 g] turbinado sugar
Scant ½ cup [100 g] unsalted butter, cut into small pieces

For the Earl Grey chocolate sauce
1 cup [225 ml] heavy cream
Scant ½ cup [100 ml] water
½ cup [100 g] superfine sugar
4 Earl Grey teabags
Heaping 1 cup [190 g] dark chocolate (70% cocoa solids), broken into small pieces

To make the chocolate sauce, put the cream, water, and sugar into a pan and heat to dissolve the sugar, then bring to a boil. Add the teabags, take off the heat, cover, and leave to infuse and cool.

Once cooled, strain the mixture into a clean pan. Bring to a boil, then remove from the heat. Immediately add the chocolate and whisk until smooth and shiny. Cover, and set aside until ready to serve.

Preheat your oven to 350°F [180°C].

For the pear compote, peel, halve, and core the pears, then cut into roughly equal-sized chunks. Heat the butter and cider in a pan until the butter has melted. Add the vanilla seeds, and stir well. Now add the pears, and cook gently for 4 minutes. Divide the pear compote between individual baking dishes, and set aside.

To make the crumble, mix the flour, ground almonds, and sugars together in a bowl, and rub in the butter with your fingertips, or pulse in a food processor, until the mixture looks like crumble.

Peel the pears for roasting, and trim a thin slice from the base of each one, so they will stand upright.

Stand a pear in the center of each baking dish. Scatter the crumble over the pear compote, and bake for 25 to 30 minutes, until golden and well-cooked. When almost ready, gently warm the chocolate sauce.

Pour the warm chocolate sauce over the pears to serve.

In 2003, on the first menu of my first restaurant, Black Pig, I set about including a chocolate dessert that would be a lifelong friend. Over the years, in times of need, this recipe has saved the day, and got me new friends! Of late, it has grown up and taken on a pastry jacket, making for a more interesting texture. I didn't want to share this recipe at first, because it's like a best friend, but having thought long and hard about it, I'd like you to reap the benefits too! I usually make individual tarts, but you could bake one big one if you prefer.

Warm chocolate tart "Black Pig"

Serves 6

For the pastry

3¼ cups [430 g] all-purpose flour, plus extra to dust

5 tsp [20 g] superfine sugar

Scant 1 tsp [4 g] fine salt

Scant ½ Tbsp [4 g] baking powder

¾ cup [170 g] unsalted butter, softened

¾ cup [180 ml] milk (approximately)

For the chocolate filling

⅔ cup [115 g] dark chocolate (70% cocoa solids), broken into small pieces

Scant ½ cup [110 g] unsalted butter, softened

Scant ⅔ cup [125 g] superfine sugar

Scant ½ cup [100 g] egg whites (about 3 large)

3⅔ Tbsp [30 g] all-purpose flour

To finish

Cocoa powder to dust

To make the pastry, mix all the dry ingredients together in a bowl. Using your fingers, rub in the butter until the mixture resembles a crumble mix. Add most of the milk and mix with a table knife to a smooth dough, adding as much of the remaining milk as you need, but don't overwork it. Wrap in plastic wrap, and chill for 1 hour.

Preheat your oven to 350°F [180°C].

Unwrap the dough and roll out on a surface lightly dusted with flour to ⅛ thick. Cut out 6 circles and use to line 6 individual 3¼-in [8 cm] tart rings placed on a baking sheet, or use the sheet of pastry to line an 8-in [20 cm] tart pan. Place in the fridge to rest for 30 minutes.

Line the pastry case(s) with a double layer of plastic wrap, and fill with baking beans. Pull the edges of the plastic wrap up and twist together to make little parcels in the pans. Bake for 15 minutes, then remove the baking bean parcel(s) and return the pastry case(s) to the oven for an additional 5 minutes. When the pastry is cooked and golden, transfer the tart case(s) to a wire rack.

To make the chocolate filling, put the chocolate and butter into a large heatproof bowl over a pan of gently simmering water, making sure the base of the bowl is not touching the water. Leave until melted, then lift the bowl from the pan. Whisk the sugar into the chocolate mixture, then whisk in the egg whites. Finally, whisk in the flour until evenly combined.

Stand the tart case(s) on a baking sheet and pour in the chocolate mixture, filling the case(s) to the top. Carefully transfer to the oven and bake for 10 minutes.

Serve straight from the oven dusted with cocoa powder, with a good dollop of clotted cream or ice cream of your choice on the side.

My good friend and chef, Pete Biggs, has been making this rice pudding for the restaurants for ages. I have to admit (through gritted teeth!) that his recipe is better than mine. Here, I'm serving it with my apple and prune compote, which is also lovely eaten simply with yogurt. Do try it with this rice pudding though… the combination is seriously good.

Pete's rice pudding with apple and prune compote

Serves 6

For the compote
1¾ cups [250 g] pitted prunes
Scant ½ cup [100 ml] brandy
Scant ½ cup [100 ml] water
½ cup [100 g] superfine sugar
Finely grated zest and juice
  of 1 lemon
½ cinnamon stick
1 vanilla bean, split
  lengthwise
7 cups peeled, cored, and
  diced (about 700 g) cooking
  apples

For the rice pudding
2⅛ cups [500 ml] whole milk
2⅛ cups [500 ml] heavy
  cream
½ tsp salt
2 vanilla beans, split
  lengthwise, and seeds
  scraped
¾ cup [150 g] short grain rice
Scant ½ cup [90 g] superfine
  sugar

To make the compote, soak the prunes in the brandy overnight. The following day, heat the water and sugar in a saucepan to dissolve the sugar, then bring to a boil. Add the lemon zest and juice, cinnamon stick and vanilla bean. Simmer for 2 minutes, then add the prunes and any remaining brandy. Bring back to a simmer, and take off the heat.

Leave until cold and then transfer the prunes, flavorings, and liquor to a sterilized Kilner or mason jar. Seal and store in a cool, dark place; the longer the prunes have to mature (up to a month), the better they will be. Leave them for at least 4 or 5 days if you can.

For the rice pudding, preheat your oven to 325°F [160°C]. Put all the ingredients into a large ovenproof pan, including the vanilla beans as well as the seeds, and stir well. Bring to a simmer over medium heat, and then take off the heat. Lay a circle of parchment paper on the surface and transfer to the oven to cook for 30 minutes.

In the meantime, put the prune compote into a pan, and add the diced apples. Stir, and bring to a simmer over low heat. Cook for a couple of minutes until the apples are just tender.

To serve, I like to put the pan of rice pudding in the center of the table with the bowl of apple and prune compote on the side, and let everyone help themselves.

To follow

Make this dessert at the beginning of the summer, when local strawberries are amazing and the hedgerows are full of elderflower. There is a bit of time involved here, but believe me, it's worth it. The sweeter the strawberries, the better it will be. The set cream and sorbet recipes are versatile, so feel free to play around with the flavors.

Elderflower cream with strawberry sorbet

Serves 6

For the elderflower cream
2 sheets of bronze leaf gelatin
Scant 2½ cups [560 ml]
  whole milk
¾ cup [180 ml] heavy cream
Scant ½ cup [90 g] superfine
  sugar
Scant ½ cup [100 ml]
  elderflower cordial

For the strawberry sorbet
2¼ lb [1 kg] strawberries
Heaping ¾ cup [175 g]
  superfine sugar
½ cup [125 ml] sparkling wine
Scant ½ cup [100 ml] liquid
  glucose

To finish
15 strawberries, hulled and
  quartered
Finely grated zest of 1 lime

For the sorbet, halve the strawberries, place in a heatproof bowl with ½ cup [100 g] of the sugar, and toss to mix. Cover the bowl with plastic wrap, then place it over a pan of boiling water for 2 hours to draw all the juice out of the strawberries.

Meanwhile, make the elderflower cream. Soak the gelatin in a shallow dish of ice water. Pour the milk and cream into a pan, add the sugar, and dissolve over medium heat, then bring to a simmer and take off the heat. Immediately drain the gelatin and add to the hot milk mixture, whisking until melted, then whisk in the elderflower cordial.

Pour the elderflower cream into 6 individual dishes or glasses, dividing the mixture evenly, and place in the fridge to set for 3 hours.

When the strawberries are ready, transfer them to a cheesecloth-lined strainer over a bowl, and squeeze to extract as much juice as possible. Weigh 4½ oz [125 g] of the strawberry pulp and 1⅛ cups [250 ml] of the strawberry juice (see note).

To make the sorbet, put the measured strawberry pulp and juice into a pan and add the sparkling wine, glucose, and remaining sugar. Bring to a simmer over medium heat, and simmer gently for 4 minutes. Allow to cool, then churn in an ice-cream machine until firm. Transfer the sorbet to a freezerproof container, and place in the freezer until ready to serve.

To assemble, gently toss the quartered strawberries with the lime zest, and spoon on top of the elderflower creams. Using a warmed ice-cream scoop or large spoon, scoop balls of the sorbet, and place on top of the strawberries and cream. Serve immediately.

Note If you have some strawberry juice left over, you can make a jelly to top the creams. Measure the juice and use 1 sheet of leaf gelatin per scant ½ cup [100 ml] juice. Soak the gelatin in cold water. Bring the strawberry juice to a simmer, squeeze the gelatin to remove excess water, and add to the juice off the heat, whisking to dissolve. Leave to cool. When on the point of setting, pour on top of the creams, and refrigerate until set before topping with the strawberries and sorbet.

My daughter, Jessica, loves to bake. Ever since I can remember, she's joined me in the kitchen at home. Of all her baking successes (and there have been many), this is the recipe that to date is the family's favorite. Why "Messy"? Well, in all my years of cooking, I've never seen anyone more accomplished in getting every surface in the kitchen and herself covered in whatever she's making. We "borrowed" this recipe from Claire Clark, my friend, and the world's best pastry chef.

Messy Jessie cookies

Makes 10

⅔ cup [150 g] unsalted butter, at room temperature
6½ Tbsp [80 g] soft light brown sugar
6½ Tbsp [80 g] granulated sugar
A pinch of sea salt
½ tsp vanilla extract
1 large egg
Heaping 1¾ cups [250 g] all-purpose flour
½ tsp baking soda
⅔ cup [100 g] dark chocolate (70% cocoa solids), chopped
⅔ cup [100 g] milk chocolate, chopped

Using an electric mixer, beat the butter, sugars, salt, and vanilla extract together until thoroughly combined. Add the egg, and beat in well.

Sift the flour and baking soda over the mixture, and mix until evenly combined. Finally, fold in the dark and milk chocolates.

Form the dough into a log, wrap in plastic wrap, and place in the fridge for 3 hours to firm up.

Preheat your oven to 350°F [180°C]. Line 2 baking sheets with baking parchment.

Divide the dough into 10 equal pieces and shape into balls. Place on the baking sheets, leaving enough room in between for spreading. Bake for 15 to 20 minutes until golden.

Leave the cookies on the sheets for a minute or two to firm up slightly, then transfer to a wire rack and leave to cool—that is, if you can resist eating them immediately.

To follow

I find meringues fascinating—the fact that simple egg whites and sugar can be whisked together to create something so special is magic, and I always have some sort of meringue dessert on my restaurant menus. I like to balance the sweetness with something sharp, hence the lemon and tangy yogurt sorbet topping for this pavlova. It's a favorite dessert at home.

Lemon curd pavlova with yogurt sorbet

Serves 6

For the meringue
3 large egg whites
¾ cup [150 g] superfine sugar
1 vanilla bean, split
   lengthwise, and seeds
   scraped
2 tsp cornstarch
2 tsp white wine vinegar

For the lemon curd
Finely grated zest of 1 lemon
Generous ½ cup [130 ml]
   lemon juice (about
   3 lemons)
½ cup [100 g] superfine sugar
Generous ⅓ cup [80 g] egg
   yolks (about 4 large)
1 egg white
7 oz [200 g] unsalted butter,
   chilled and diced

For the yogurt sorbet
⅞ cup [200 ml] whole milk
½ cup [100 g] superfine sugar
½ cup [120 ml] liquid glucose
Scant 1½ cups [300 g] full-fat
   Greek yogurt

For the lemon syrup
⅞ cup [200 ml] liquid glucose
Finely grated zest of 1 lemon
Scant ½ cup [100 ml] lemon
   juice
½ cup [100 g] superfine sugar

To finish
⅔ cup [50 g] slivered
   almonds, toasted

Preheat your oven to 225°F [110°C] and line a baking sheet with a silicone mat or baking parchment. Wipe your stand mixer (or other large) bowl with paper towels dipped in vinegar to remove any trace of grease.

Using a stand mixer, or electric hand mixer, whisk the egg whites in the bowl to soft peaks. Whisk in the sugar a third at a time, until fully incorporated; add the vanilla seeds with the last of the sugar. Gently fold in the cornstarch and wine vinegar, using a spatula or large metal spoon.

Using a large spoon, shape the meringue into 6 equal-sized mounds on the prepared sheet and then use the back of the spoon to make an indent in each one. Bake the meringues for 1 hour.

Meanwhile, make the lemon curd. Whisk the lemon zest and juice, sugar, egg yolks, and egg white in a heatproof bowl over a pan of simmering water, until the mixture thickens. Remove the bowl from the pan, and whisk in the cold butter, a piece at a time, until it is all incorporated. Strain through a strainer into a bowl, cover, and refrigerate until set.

To make the yogurt sorbet, put the milk, sugar, and liquid glucose into a pan, and place over medium heat to dissolve the sugar. Bring to a simmer, take off the heat, and leave to cool. Once cold, whisk in the yogurt, then transfer to an ice-cream machine and churn until thick.

For the lemon syrup, heat the glucose, lemon zest and juice, and the sugar in a pan over medium heat to dissolve the sugar. Let simmer for 3 minutes, then pour the syrup into a bowl, and leave to cool.

When the sorbet is ready, spoon into a suitable container and place in the freezer. When the meringues are baked, transfer to a wire rack to cool.

To assemble, put a spoonful of lemon curd in the center of each bowl and place a meringue on top. Drizzle the lemon syrup over the meringues and around each plate. Top each meringue with a scoop of the sorbet. Scatter over the toasted almonds, and serve, with an extra spoonful of lemon curd on the side, if you like.

I know a lot of people find treacle tart overly sweet. My filling includes molasses, salt, and citrus flavors to take the edge off the sweetness, and the raspberries balance the flavors beautifully. You can have ice cream with it if you like, but for me, it has to be clotted or pouring cream. It's easier to make a larger quantity of pastry and it freezes well—so I've given enough here to make two tarts.

Treacle and raspberry tart

Serves 6

For the sweet pastry

7 oz [200 g] unsalted butter, diced
1¼ cups [180 g] confectioners' sugar
1 large egg
¾ cup [140 g] egg yolks (about 8 to 10 large)
3¾ cups [500 g] all-purpose flour, plus extra to dust

For the filling

Scant ¾ cup [225 g] golden syrup or light corn syrup
Heaping 2 Tbsp [50 g] molasses
Scant 1 cup [220 ml] heavy cream
½ tsp coarse sea salt
Finely grated zest of 1 orange
Finely grated zest of 1 lemon
Juice of ½ lemon
1¼ cups [75 g] fresh white bread crumbs
2 large eggs, beaten
¾ cup [100 g] raspberries, plus extra to serve

To make the pastry, using a stand mixer or electric hand mixer, cream the butter and confectioners' sugar together in a bowl until pale and fluffy. Lightly beat the egg and egg yolks in a separate bowl. Gradually beat the egg into the creamed mixture. Once it is all incorporated, add the flour. Stop mixing as soon as it forms a dough.

Tip the dough out onto a surface dusted lightly with flour, and knead briefly until smooth. Divide in half, shape each piece into a ball, and flatten to a disc. Wrap in plastic wrap. Chill one portion in the fridge for 1 hour; freeze the other for a future tart.

Preheat your oven to 350°F [180°C].

Roll out the pastry on a lightly floured surface to ⅛ in [3 mm] thick, and use to line a loose-bottomed rectangular tart pan, about 10-by-4-by-1¼-in [25-by-10-cm-by-3-cm deep], or a 7 in [18 cm] round tart pan, 1¼ in [3 cm] deep, leaving any excess overhanging the rim. Place in the fridge to rest for 30 minutes.

Line the pastry case with a double layer of plastic wrap, and fill with baking beans. Bring the edges of the plastic wrap up and twist together to make a parcel. Bake for 15 minutes, then remove the baking bean parcel, and return the pastry case to the oven for an additional 5 minutes, until golden and baked. Place on a wire rack to cool.

To make the filling, put the golden syrup, molasses, cream, salt, citrus zests, and lemon juice into a heavy-bottomed pan, and stir over medium heat, until the mixture is smooth and very hot. Take the pan off the heat, and add the bread crumbs and beaten eggs. Mix until evenly combined.

Spoon the filling into the pastry case and add the raspberries, distributing them evenly. Bake for 15 minutes, until the filling is just set in the center. Place on a wire rack to cool, trimming away the excess pastry from the rim while the tart is still just warm.

Cut the tart into slices and serve just warm, or at room temperature, with extra raspberries on the side and clotted cream or pouring cream.

This recipe is inspired by nostalgic memories of ice-cream sandwiches my Mum would make with Neapolitan ice cream bought from the ice cream man. I'd like to think my take is an improvement!

Passion fruit and toasted coconut ice-cream sandwich

Serves 6

For the ice cream
1¼ cups [300 ml] fresh
   passion fruit juice (from
   about 20 passion fruit)
3 sheets of bronze leaf gelatin
Scant 1¾ cups [400 ml] heavy
   cream
5 large egg yolks
Scant ⅔ cup [120 g] superfine
   sugar
Heaping 1⅛ cups [260 g] full-
   fat cream cheese,
   at room temperature

For the coconut cookie
¾ cup [55 g] grated dried
   coconut
½ cup [100 g] egg whites
   (about 3 large)
½ cup [100 g] superfine sugar
¾ cup [100 g] all-purpose
   flour

For the coconut yogurt
Scant ¾ cup [50 g] grated
   dried coconut
Scant 1½ cups [300 g] full-fat
   Greek yogurt
Finely grated zest of 1 lime
3½ Tbsp [30 g] confectioners'
   sugar

For the passion fruit syrup
Generous ⅓ cup [80 g]
   passion fruit pulp (from
   about 4 scooped-out
   passion fruit)
¼ cup [50 g] superfine sugar

For the ice cream, pour the passion fruit juice into a large pan, and bring to a simmer over medium heat. Let bubble to reduce by three-quarters, then take off the heat. Soak the gelatin in a dish of ice water.

Add the cream to the reduced passion fruit juice, and return to a simmer. Meanwhile, whisk the egg yolks and sugar together in a bowl. Pour on the hot passion fruit cream, whisking as you do so. While it is still very hot, squeeze the excess water from the gelatin, then add to the mixture, whisking to melt completely. Let cool, then cover and refrigerate until set.

Once the mixture is cold, whisk in the cream cheese. Spoon into a piping bag and pipe into 6 individual rectangular molds. Freeze until firm.

To make the cookie, preheat your oven to 350°F [180°C] and the broiler to medium-high. Scatter the dried coconut on a broiler pan, and broil until golden, stirring every 2 minutes to color evenly. Let cool.

Line a baking sheet with a silicone mat. Whisk the egg whites and sugar together in a bowl until evenly mixed. Add the toasted coconut and flour, and stir to combine. Using an icing spatula, spread the mixture thinly and evenly on the baking sheet. Bake for 8 to 10 minutes until golden all over.

When you take the baking sheet from the oven, mark your desired cookie shapes with a sharp knife. Once cooled, they should snap where marked, with a little help. Keep in an airtight container until ready to assemble.

For the coconut yogurt, toast the coconut as above, and let cool. Once cooled, add to the yogurt with the lime zest and confectioners' sugar, and stir until evenly combined. Set aside in the fridge until ready to serve.

For the syrup, heat the passion fruit pulp and sugar in a pan over medium heat to dissolve the sugar. Bring to a simmer, reduce the heat slightly, and cook until reduced to a syrupy consistency. Leave to cool.

To assemble, unmold the ice creams and sandwich each one between two coconut cookies. Serve immediately, with the passion fruit syrup spooned over, and a dollop of coconut yogurt on the side.

BASICS

Lemon oil

**Makes about 1¾ cups
[400 ml]**

Finely pared zest of 5
  unwaxed lemons
1¼ cups [300 ml] light canola oil
100ml light olive oil

Put the pared zest of 4 lemons into a blender with the oils and blitz for 2 minutes. Pour the oil mixture into a pitcher, and leave to infuse and settle for 24 hours. Decant the oil into a sterilized bottle, and add the pared zest of the remaining lemon. Keep in the fridge and use within a month.

Horseradish and lemon oil Add ⅓ cup 75g grated fresh horseradish to the blender with the other ingredients.

Orange oil

**Makes about 1¾ cups
[400 ml]**

Finely pared zest of 4 oranges
1¼ cups [300 ml] light canola oil
100ml light olive oil

Put all of the ingredients into a blender and blitz for 2 minutes. Pour the oil mixture into a pitcher and leave to infuse and settle for 24 hours. Decant the oil into a sterilized bottle. Keep in the fridge and use within a month.

Basil oil

**Makes about ⅔ cup
[150 ml]**

1 cup [30 g] basil leaves
1 cup [30 g] flat-leaf parsley
  leaves
⅔ cup [150 ml] light olive oil
Cornish sea salt

Bring a pan of salted water to a simmer, and get a bowl of ice water ready. When the water is simmering, add the herbs, and blanch for 30 seconds. Immediately scoop out the herbs, and plunge them straight into the ice water to cool quickly. Drain, and squeeze out excess water.

Put the blanched herbs into a blender with the olive oil and blitz for 2 minutes. Transfer the mixture to a container, cover, and refrigerate for at least 3 to 4 hours, preferably overnight.

Warm the oil slightly, then pass it through a strainer into a clean bottle. The oil is now ready to use. It will keep in the fridge for a week.

Chili oil

**Makes about 1¾ cups
[400 ml]**

2 green chiles, chopped (seeds
  left in)
1¾ cups [400 ml] light canola oil

Put the chiles and oil into a saucepan. Warm over medium heat—until the oil is just too hot to put your finger in. Remove from the heat, and pour the oil and chiles into a food processor. Blend for 2 minutes, then pour the liquid into a container and leave to cool.

Once cold, strain the oil into a clean bottle, and store in the fridge until needed. It will keep in the fridge for a week.

Curry oil

**Makes about 1¾ cups
[400 ml]**

4 tsp mild curry powder
1¾ cups [400 ml] light canola oil

Sprinkle the curry powder into a dry skillet, and toast over medium heat for 1 to 2 minutes until it releases its aroma; don't let it burn. Pour the oil into the skillet, and immediately remove from the heat. Give it a good stir, and then pour it into a pitcher.

Leave to infuse and settle for 24 hours, then decant the curry oil into a sterilized bottle. It will keep for 3 months in a dark cupboard.

Fish stock

Makes about 2⅛ cups
[500 ml]

2¼ lb [1 kg] turbot, flounder,
or sole bones and/or cod
heads, washed and all blood
removed

Preheat your oven to 400°F [200°C]. Line a roasting pan with silicone paper and lay the fish bones and/or cod heads in it. Roast for 30 minutes, then turn the bones over, and roast for another 10 minutes.

Transfer the roasted bones to a stockpot, and pour on enough water to cover. Bring to a simmer over medium heat, and skim off any impurities from the surface. Simmer for 30 minutes, then take off the heat, and strain through a strainer into another pan. Bring the stock back to a simmer, and reduce by half. Remove from the heat, and allow to cool.

The stock is now ready to use. You can store it in the fridge for up to 3 days, or freeze it for up to 2 months.

Chicken stock

Makes about 2⅛ cups
[500 ml]

4½ lb [2 kg] chicken bones

Preheat your oven to 400°F [200°C]. Place all the bones in a roasting pan and roast for 30 minutes, then turn them over, and roast for another 30 minutes.

Transfer the bones to a stockpot, and pour on enough water to cover. Bring to a boil, and simmer for 3 hours, skimming the surface regularly. Pass the stock through a strainer into another pan. Bring back to a simmer, and reduce by half. Remove from the heat, and allow to cool.

The stock is now ready to use. You can store it in the fridge for up to 3 days, or freeze it for up to 2 months.

Vegetable stock

Makes about 8½ cups [2 L]

2 onions, peeled and minced
6 carrots, pared and finely
  chopped
6 celery stalks, finely chopped
2 leeks, trimmed, washed,
  and finely sliced
2 garlic cloves, peeled and
  crushed
10 white peppercorns
2 star anise
2 tsp fennel seeds
Pinch of sea salt
2⅛ cups [500 ml] dry
  white wine
1 thyme sprig
A handful of parsley stalks

Put all of the vegetables, the garlic, spices, and salt into a large saucepan, and pour on enough water to cover. Bring to a simmer over medium heat. Simmer for 30 minutes, and then remove from the heat. Pour the wine into the stock, and add the herbs. Leave to cool.

For best results, leave overnight in the fridge before straining the stock to remove the vegetables, spices, and herbs. The stock is now ready to use. It can be frozen for up to 2 months.

Mayonnaise

Makes about 1½ cups [350 ml]

3 egg yolks
1 tsp English mustard
Juice of ½ lemon, or 2 tsp white wine vinegar, or cider vinegar
1¼ cups [300 ml] light canola oil
Sea salt and freshly ground black pepper

Put the egg yolks, mustard, and lemon juice or wine (or cider) vinegar into a bowl, and whisk together for 1 minute. Now slowly add the oil, drop by drop to begin with, then in a thin, steady stream, whisking constantly, until the mixture is emulsified and thick. (Or you can make the mayonnaise in a blender or food processor, blending the egg yolks, mustard, and lemon juice or vinegar for 1 minute, and then adding the oil in a thin, steady stream through the funnel with the motor running.)

Season the mayonnaise with salt and pepper to taste. Cover, and refrigerate until needed. It will keep in the fridge for a couple of days.

Herb mayonnaise Add 3 to 4 Tbsp chopped herbs to the finished mayonnaise. Dill, tarragon, and parsley are good options with fish.

Spicy anchovy mayonnaise Put 2 egg yolks, a pinch of saffron strands, 2 chopped garlic cloves, 1 minced seeded chile, 4 salted anchovies in oil, and the juice of ½ lemon into a blender or small food processor, and blitz for 1 minute. With the motor running, slowly add 1¾ cups [400 ml] olive oil through the funnel. Season the mayonnaise, scrape into a bowl, cover, and refrigerate as above.

Tomato ketchup

Makes 1½ cups [400 ml]; serves 10 to 12

A drizzle of olive oil
2 red onions, peeled and chopped
6 garlic cloves, peeled and sliced
20 black peppercorns
5½ lb [2.5 kg] ripe tomatoes, roughly chopped
½ cup [100 g] superfine sugar
4 tsp chopped thyme
1 cinnamon stick
4 bay leaves
1¼ cups [300 ml] red wine vinegar
Sea salt and freshly ground black pepper

Heat a large saucepan over medium heat, and add the olive oil. When hot, add the onions and garlic, and cook for 2 minutes until the onions start to turn translucent.

Meanwhile, tie the peppercorns in a piece of cheesecloth and add to the pan with the tomatoes, sugar, thyme, cinnamon, and bay leaves. Cook for 15 minutes, until the tomatoes have broken down. Continue to cook until the tomato liquid has reduced right down, almost to nothing. Now add the wine vinegar, and let bubble for 5 minutes.

Remove the cinnamon, bay, and peppercorn bundle. Transfer the contents of the pan to a blender or food processor, and blend until smooth, then pass though a strainer into a bowl. Taste for seasoning, adding salt and pepper as required.

Transfer to a clean container and allow to cool, then seal. The tomato ketchup will keep in the fridge for up to a week; or you can freeze it for up to a month.

Index

A

aïoli, roasted garlic 178
ale-cured salmon 60
almonds: almond and sherry vinegar
    bread sauce174
    almond cream 198
    pear crumble 200
anchovy mayonnaise 52, 219
angels on horseback 169
apples: apple and prune compote 204
    gin-cured sea (steelhead) trout with
      apple and fennel 56
    pickled mackerel with red cabbage,
      apple, and cider 76
    raw mackerel with apple, celery, and
      bacon 58
    shallot, caper, and apple relish 66
arugula and black olive salad 79
asparagus: chilled asparagus soup 86
    John Dory, shaved asparagus, chile,
      and orange salad 138
    smoked salmon, cauliflower, and
      asparagus bake 163
avocados: octopus, avocado, and
    tomato salad 120
    a simple bass ceviche 72

B

bacon: angels on horseback 169
    cod, bacon, kale, and parsnip salad
      140
    hake with bacon, hazelnuts, and leeks
      189
    monkfish, bean, and bacon stew 109
    raw mackerel with apple, celery, and
      bacon 58
    see also pancetta
barbecue sauce 190
barbecued jerk lobster 172
barbecued langoustines 176
basil: basil and ginger crème fraîche 63
    basil and orange mayonnaise 38
    basil dressing 130
    basil oil 216
Basque potatoes 193
bass 10
    bass with air-dried ham, zucchini,
      lemon, and herbs 180
    a simple bass ceviche 72
beans see cannellini beans
béarnaise butter 152
beef: cod and ox cheek stew 114

beet chutney 63
Belgian endive, creamed 100
bottarga: poached eggs with bottarga
    and salmon roe 41
brandade, smoked 31
bread: pepper and shallot flatbreads 156
bread sauce, almond and sherry
    vinegar 174
brill, citrus-cured 52
    see also turbot
butter: béarnaise butter 152
    green sauce butter 177
    saffron and olive butter 166
    smoked paprika and cilantro
      butter 146
    spiced butter dressing 184
    watercress and anise butter 148
buying and storing seafood 10–11

C

cabbage see red cabbage
cannellini beans: hot marinated lemon
    sole 82
    monkfish, bean, and bacon stew 109
    romesco sauce 116
carrots: carrot and fennel chutney 70
    pickled vegetables 69
cauliflower: cauliflower pickle 188
    smoked salmon, cauliflower, and
      asparagus bake 163
    squid, watercress and cauliflower
      salad 123
celeriac: celeriac chips 46
    celeriac pickle 46
    raw scallops, celeriac broth, and green
      chili oil 46
celery, pickled 58
ceviche, bass 72
chanterelles, red mullet (goatfish) with
    178
cheese: my fish pie 158
    scallops with Cheddar crumbs 146
    smoked salmon, cauliflower, and
      asparagus bake 163
    see also cream cheese
chicken stock 218
chickpeas: squid curry 110
    stuffed squid, red peppers, chickpeas,
      olives, and sherry 151
chiles: barbecue sauce 190
    chili jam 28
    chili oil 216

jalapeño mayonnaise 36
jalapeño yogurt 70
John Dory, shaved asparagus, chile,
    and orange salad 138
    shrimp, chile and potato salad 126
    raw scallops, celeriac broth, and green
      chili oil 46
    tomato and chile chutney 176
chips, celeriac 46
chocolate: Earl Grey chocolate sauce 200
    Messy Jessie cookies 206
    warm chocolate tart "Black Pig" 203
chowder, clam and shrimp 91
chutney: beet 63
    carrot and fennel 70
    tomato and chile 176
cider: cider-pickled oysters 66
    mussels with sage, cider, and clotted
      cream 99
    pickled mackerel with red cabbage,
      apple, and cider 76
cilantro: ginger and cilantro yogurt 188
    lime and cilantro dressing 120
    tomato and cilantro salad 144
citrus-cured brill 52
clams 11
    clam and shrimp chowder 91
    razor clam and scallop soup 96
    razor clams, carrot and fennel
      chutney, jalapeño yogurt 70
cockles 11
    cockle and seaweed risotto 104
coconut: coconut rice 172
    coconut yogurt 59, 212
    passion fruit and toasted coconut ice-
      cream sandwich 212
    razor clam and scallop soup 96
cod: cod and ox cheek stew 114
    cod, bacon, kale and parsnip salad 140
    my fish pie 158
cod roe dip 34
cookies, Messy Jessie 206
corn: corn, red onion, and tomato
    relish 36
    corn soup with scallops and pickled
      onions 90
Cornish style of smoked brandade 31
court bouillon 133
crab 10
    chilled asparagus soup 86
    crab and saffron pasta bake 162
    crab and tomato salad 124

crab pâté with pink grapefruit 20
crab Scotch quail eggs 22
crab with tomatoes, chili, green
    peppercorns, and herbs 102
cream: elderflower cream 205
    salad cream 60, 76, 133
cream cheese: hot-smoked salmon
    pâté 32
    pea pâté 169
crème fraîche: basil and ginger crème
    fraîche 63
    lemon crème fraîche 198
crumble, pear 200
cucumber: cucumber and mint dipping
    sauce 25
    cucumber and mint relish 37
    cucumber and seaweed salad 60
curry: curry-cured mullet 59
    curry oil 216
    squid curry 110
    smoked haddock and curried lentils 161
squid 11
    squid curry 110

D
dip, Jacob's favorite cod roe 34
Doom Bar marinated seafood 69
English sole, hot soused 81
dressings: basil 130
    cashew and lime 136
    grape 54
    horseradish 124
    lemon 134
    lime and cilantro 120
    orange and tarragon 100
    red onion, orange and tarragon 78
    spiced butter 184

E
Earl Grey chocolate sauce 200
eggplant: eggplant salad 130
    squid curry 110
eggs: crab Scotch quail eggs 22
    poached eggs with bottarga and
        salmon roe 41
    smoked haddock soup with poached
        egg and pancetta 94
elderflower cream 205
equipment 12–13

F
fennel: carrot and fennel chutney 70
    fennel, gherkin, and olive salad 194
    gin-cured sea (steelhead) trout with
        apple and fennel 56
    monkfish on the bone, spiced butter
        and fennel 184
    mullet with fennel, lime, and orange 74

pickled vegetables 69
fish finger roll 42
fish pie 158
fish stew 106
fish stock 218
flatbreads, pepper and shallot 156
fritters, pancetta-wrapped oyster 25

G
garlic: roasted garlic aïoli 178
gherkins: fennel, gherkin, and olive
    salad 194
gin-cured sea (steelhead) trout with
    apple and fennel 56
ginger: basil and ginger crème fraîche 63
    ginger and cilantro yogurt 188
    ginger-cured mackerel 63
grape dressing 54
grapefruit: crab pâté with pink
    grapefruit 20
green sauce butter 177

H
haddock: fish finger roll 42
    haddock baked in a bag with
        béarnaise butter 152
    see also smoked haddock
hake with bacon, hazelnuts, and leeks
    189
ham: bass with air-dried ham, zucchini,
    lemon, and herbs 180
hazelnuts: hake with bacon, hazelnuts,
    and leeks 189
herb mayonnaise 128
herrings, pickled 78
hollandaise: lime hollandaise 154
    smoked hollandaise sauce 170
horseradish: horseradish dressing 124
    horseradish mash 41
    raw salmon with vodka, orange, and
        horseradish 48

I
ice cream: passion fruit and toasted
    coconut ice-cream sandwich 212

J
Jacob's favorite cod roe dip 34
jalapeño mayonnaise 36
jalapeño yogurt 70
jelly, pink grapefruit 20
jerk lobster 172
Joe's kedgeree 112
John Dory, shaved asparagus, chile and
    orange salad 138

K
kale: cod, bacon, kale, and parsnip
    salad 140

kedgeree, Joe's 112
ketchup: red pepper ketchup 79
    tomato ketchup 219
kohlrabi tartare salad 133

L
langoustines: barbecued langoustines
    176
    langoustines with saffron and olive
        butter 166
leeks: hake with bacon, hazelnuts and
    leeks 189
lemon: citrus-cured brill 52
    lemon crème fraîche 198
    lemon curd pavlova 208
    lemon dressing 134
    lemon oil 216
lemon sole: hot marinated lemon sole
    with pickled onions and grapes 82
    lemon sole, green sauce butter 177
lentils: smoked haddock and curried
    lentils 161
limes: lime and cilantro dressing 120
    lime hollandaise 154
    lime yogurt 161
    a simple bass ceviche 72
lobster 11
    barbecued jerk lobster 172
    dressed lobster with herb
        mayonnaise 128
    lobster risotto balls 38

M
mackerel: ginger-cured mackerel 63
    mackerel and noodle salad 136
    mackerel with barbecue sauce 190
    pickled mackerel with red cabbage,
        apple, and cider 76
    raw mackerel with apple, celery, and
        bacon 58
    see also smoked mackerel
mayonnaise 219
    anchovy 52
    basil and orange 38
    herb 128
    jalapeño 36
    pea and mint 42
    roasted garlic aïoli 178
    watercress 22
meringue: lemon curd pavlova 208
Messy Jessie cookies 206
monkfish: monkfish, bean, and bacon
    stew 109
    monkfish on the bone, spiced butter,
        and fennel 184
    monkfish satay 186
    monkfish, cauliflower pickle, ginger
        and cilantro yogurt 188

verjus-cured monkfish 54
mullet: crispy fried mullet 28
  curry-cured mullet 59
  mullet with fennel, lime, and orange
    74
  red mullet (goatfish) and mushroom
    miso broth 92
  red mullet (goatfish) with chanterelles
    178
mushrooms: hot soused English sole 81
  mussels 10, 11
  mussels with sage, cider, and clotted
    cream 99
my fish pie 158
my fish stew 106

N
noodles: mackerel and noodle salad 136
  shrimp noodle soup 89
nutrition 10
nuts: zucchini and nut salad 134
  see also almonds; hazelnuts etc

O
octopus 11
  braised octopus with romesco
    sauce 116
  octopus, avocado, and tomato
    salad 120
  seared octopus, almond and sherry
    vinegar bread sauce 174
oil: basil 216
  chili 216
  curry 216
  lemon 216
  orange 216
  seaweed 86
  shiso 92
oily fish 10, 11, 15
olives: arugula and black olive salad 79
  fennel, gherkin and olive salad 194
  langoustines with saffron and olive
    butter 166
  raw tuna with green olive sauce 51
  stuffed squid, red peppers,
    chickpeas, olives and sherry 151
onions: pickled onions 82, 90
  corn, red onion, and tomato relish 36
  red onion, orange, and tarragon
    dressing 78
oranges: barbecue sauce 190
  basil and orange mayonnaise 38
  John Dory, shaved asparagus, chilli
    and orange salad 138
  mullet with fennel, lime, and orange
    74
  orange and tarragon dressing 100

orange oil 216
raw salmon with vodka, orange, and
  horseradish 48
red onion, orange, and tarragon
  dressing 78
ox cheek: cod and ox cheek stew 114
oysters 10, 11
  angels on horseback 169
  baked oysters with watercress and
    anise butter 148
  cider-pickled oysters 66
  fried oyster roll 37
  oysters with smoked hollandaise
    sauce 170
  pancetta-wrapped oyster fritters 25

P
pairing wine with seafood 15
pancetta: pancetta-wrapped oyster
    fritters 25
  smoked haddock soup with poached
    egg and pancetta 94
paprika: smoked paprika and cilantro
    butter 146
  smoked paprika sardines 182
parsley soup, smoked mackerel,
    horseradish and lemon oil 97
parsnips: cod, bacon, kale, and parsnip
    salad 140
passion fruit and toasted coconut ice-
    cream sandwich 212
pasta: crab and saffron pasta bake 162
pastry, sweet 210
pâtés: crab 20
  hot-smoked salmon 32
  pea 169
pavlova, lemon curd 208
peanut sauce 186
pear crumble 200
peas: pea and mint mayonnaise 42
  pea pâté 169
peppers: Basque potatoes 193
  chili jam 28
  marinated pepper salad 182
  pepper and shallot flatbreads 156
  pickled peppers 59
  red pepper ketchup 79
  romesco sauce 116
  stuffed squid, red peppers, chickpeas,
    olives, and sherry 151
Pete's rice pudding 204
pickles: celeriac pickle 46
  cider-pickled oysters 66
  pickled celery 58
  pickled herrings 78
  pickled mackerel with red cabbage,
    apple, and cider 76

pickled onions 82, 90
pickled peppers 59
pickled vegetable salad 141
pickled vegetables 69
pie, fish 158
polenta coated sea robin 36
porgy 10
potatoes: Basque potatoes 193
  clam and shrimp chowder 91
  a Cornish style of smoked brandade 31
  horseradish mash 41
  my fish pie 158
  shrimp, chile, and potato salad 126
prunes: apple and prune compote 204

Q
quail eggs: crab Scotch quail eggs 22
quiche, shrimp cocktail 26

R
raspberries: treacle and raspberry
    tart 210
razor clams: razor clam and scallop
    soup 96
  razor clams, carrot and fennel
    chutney, jalapeño yogurt 70
red cabbage, pickled mackerel with 76
red mullet (goatfish): red mullet and
    eggplant salad 130
  red mullet and mushroom miso
    broth 92
  red mullet with chanterelles 178
relishes: corn, red onion, and tomato 36
  cucumber and mint 37
  shallot, caper, and apple 66
rhubarb sponge 198
rice: cockle and seaweed risotto 104
  coconut rice 172
  Joe's kedgeree 112
  lobster risotto balls 38
  Pete's rice pudding 204
roe see bottarga; cod roe; salmon roe
romesco sauce 116

S
saffron: crab and saffron pasta bake 162
  langoustines with saffron and olive
    butter 166
salad cream 60, 76, 133
salads: arugula and black olive 79
  cod, bacon, kale, and parsnip 140
  crab and tomato 124
  cucumber and seaweed 60
  eggplant 130
  fennel, gherkin and olive 194
  John Dory, shaved asparagus, chilli
    and orange 138

kohlrabi tartare 133
mackerel and noodle 136
marinated pepper 182
octopus, avocado and tomato 120
pickled vegetable 141
shrimp, chile, and potato salad 126
squid, watercress, and cauliflower
    with salami 123
tomato and cilantro 144
salami: squid, watercress, and
    cauliflower salad 123
salmon: ale-cured salmon 60
    my fish pie 158
    raw salmon with vodka, orange, and
        horseradish 48
    salmon and kohlrabi tartare salad 133
    see also smoked salmon
salmon roe, poached eggs with bottarga
    and 41
salt and seaweed baked shrimp 144
sardines: sardines with zucchini and nut
    salad 134
    sardine, pepper and shallot flatbreads
        156
    smoked paprika sardines 182
sauces: almond and sherry vinegar
    bread sauce 174
    barbecue sauce 190
    cucumber and mint dipping sauce 25
    Earl Grey chocolate sauce 200
    lime hollandaise 154
    peanut sauce 186
    red pepper ketchup 79
    romesco sauce 116
    smoked hollandaise sauce 170
scallops 11
    corn soup with scallops 90
    pan-fried scallops, creamed Belgian
        endive, orange and tarragon
        dressing 100
    raw scallops, celeriac broth, and green
        chili oil 46
    razor clam and scallop soup 96
    scallops with Cheddar crumbs 146
Scotch quail eggs 22
sea robin: sea robin with fennel,
    gherkin, and olive salad 194
    polenta coated sea robin 36
    soused sea robin 79
sea (steelhead) trout: gin-cured sea trout
    with apple and fennel 56
seafood: buying and storing 11
seafood, Doom Bar marinated 69
seaweed: cockle and seaweed risotto 104
    salt and seaweed baked shrimp 144
    seaweed oil 86
    turbot fillets, seaweed crust 154

shallot, caper, and apple relish 66
shiso oil 92
shrimp: clam and shrimp chowder 91
    shrimp, chile, and potato salad 126
    shrimp cocktail quiche 26
    shrimp noodle soup 89
    salt and seaweed baked shrimp 144
smoked haddock: a Cornish style of
    smoked brandade 31
    Joe's kedgeree 112
    my fish pie 158
    smoked haddock and curried
        lentils 161
    smoked haddock soup with poached
        egg and pancetta 94
smoked mackerel: parsley soup, smoked
    mackerel, horseradish, and lemon
    oil 97
    smoked mackerel and pickled
        vegetable salad 141
smoked salmon: hot-smoked salmon
    pâté 32
    smoked salmon, cauliflower, and
        asparagus bake 163
sole: hot marinated lemon sole with
    pickled onions and grapes 82
    hot soused English sole 81
sorbets: strawberry 205
    yogurt 208
soups: chilled asparagus soup 86
    clam and shrimp chowder 91
    corn soup with scallops and pickled
        onions 90
    parsley soup, smoked mackerel 97
    razor clam and scallop soup 96
    red mullet (goatfish) and mushroom
        miso broth 92
    shrimp noodle soup 89
    smoked haddock soup with poached
        egg and pancetta 94
soused dishes: hot soused English sole
    81
    soused sea robin 79
spinach: squid curry 110
squid 11
    squid, watercress, and cauliflower
        salad 123
    stuffed squid, red peppers, chickpeas,
        olives and sherry 151
stews: cod and ox cheek 114
    monkfish, bean, and bacon 109
    my fish stew 106
stock: chicken 218
    fish 218
    vegetable 218
strawberry sorbet 205
swordfish 10

T
tarts: shrimp cocktail quiche 26
    treacle and raspberry tart 210
    warm chocolate tart "Black Pig" 203
tomatoes: barbecue sauce 190
    chili jam 28
    corn, red onion, and tomato relish 36
    crab and tomato salad 124
    crab with tomatoes, chili, green
        peppercorns, and herbs 102
    octopus, avocado, and tomato
        salad 120
    red pepper ketchup 79
    romesco sauce 116
    shrimp cocktail quiche 26
    simple bass ceviche 72
    squid curry 110
    tomato and chili chutney 176
    tomato and cilantro salad 144
    tomato ketchup 219
tools 12–13
treacle and raspberry tart 210
tuna: raw tuna with green olive sauce 51
turbot 10
    turbot fillets, seaweed crust 154
    turbot "Getaria" 193

V
vegetables: pickled vegetable salad 141
    vegetable stock 218
    see also peppers, potatoes etc
verjus-cured monkfish 54
vodka: raw salmon with vodka, orange,
    and horseradish 48

W
watercress: squid, watercress, and
    cauliflower salad 123
    watercress and anise butter 148
    watercress mayonnaise 22
whiskey jelly 32
white fish 10, 15
why eat fish and shellfish? 10
wine, pairing with seafood 14–15

Y
yogurt: coconut yogurt 59, 212
    ginger and cilantro yogurt 188
    jalapeño yogurt 70
    lime yogurt 161
    yogurt sorbet 208

Z
zucchini:bass with air-dried ham,
    zucchini, lemon, and herbs 180
    zucchini and nut salad 134

Dedication

This book is dedicated to Joseph Tyers, a talented young chef who was taken too early from our stoves but lives on in our kitchens. Joe, you will never be forgotten. X

Acknowledgements

I genuinely feel like the luckiest chef alive. The family that surrounds me is the reason I am here and allows me the time to write this book.

Rachel, as always my rock and my best friend. Love you Chicken! Jacob and Jessica, my now not-so-little monkeys, I love you too. And Bud, the Lurcher, who is still making me smile, whatever time of day or night.

Dad, thanks for being Dad.

Mum, thanks for typing all my scribbles and decoding my writing. I couldn't have done it without you.

Ashley Outlaw, thanks for helping with the prep!

Chris Simpson, thank you for all your support and friendship. Your help with this book has been invaluable. Tim Barnes, you continue to be there pushing on and helping. Cheers!

The team in the RNO kitchen: thanks for all your hard work.

Stephi and Damon Little, your loyalty and support is always appreciated.

Ian Dodgson and Anna Davey. You two are 'strong'! The help and support you give me is amazing. Thank you.

Karl Lucking, Dawn Harman and Gilberto Giorgiano, thanks for your hard work out the front at RNO.

Also Tom Brown, Jorge Monteiro, Christian Sharp, Emma Meech, Kelly Parsons, Felix Graft, Phil Ferguson, Julie Harman, Ace Kennedy, Rosie Kimbrell, thanks to all of you.

At Outlaw's Fish Kitchen, a big thank you to Megan Rees and Simon Davies for keeping things sailing calmly, backed up by Deano Medlen (mini me) and Laura Sloan. Cheers!

At Outlaw's at The Capital I'd like to thank Pete Biggs, Sharon McArthur, Dennis Easton and their teams for their continued loyalty and support. And I'm grateful to the Levin family for giving me the opportunity to show what I can do in the big city.

At The Mariners pub, thank you to Zack, PJ, Sam, Max, Neil Kelly, Deniz, Lewis and the rest of the team. And to Sharp's Brewery for partnering up, and Ed for making it happen in the first place.

David Hunter, I really appreciate your spreadsheet support. Danny Madigan, I'm grateful for all your help, too. Also thanks to Chris Prindl for making my wonderful plates.

At Quadrille, thanks to Helen Lewis for the creative vision and on-going support on the third book together.

To my editor, Janet Illsley, who must think I don't know what the word 'deadline' means… sorry, but a massive thanks!

David Loftus, for once again making my food look fantastic with his camera. It's such an honour to work with you.

Jamie Oliver, thank you from the bottom of my heart for writing such a lovely foreword. It means so much.

And a final thanks to you for buying, borrowing or stealing this book! I hope it brings you lots of fun…

Publishing director Sarah Lavelle
Creative director Helen Lewis
Project editor Janet Illsley
Design concept and illustration Arielle Gamble
Designer Emily Lapworth
Photography David Loftus
Food for photography Nathan Outlaw
Production Emily Noto, Vincent Smith

First published in 2016 by Quadrille Publishing Limited
www.quadrille.com

Cataloguing in Publication Data: a catalogue record for this book is available from the British Library.

ISBN 978 184949 915 6

Printed in China